OECD Reviews on Local Job Creation

Employment and Skills Strategies in Turkey

This work is published under the responsibility of the Secretary-General of the OECD. The opinions expressed and arguments employed herein do not necessarily reflect the official views of OECD member countries.

This document, as well as any data and any map included herein, are without prejudice to the status of or sovereignty over any territory, to the delimitation of international frontiers and boundaries and to the name of any territory, city or area.

Please cite this publication as:
OECD (2017), *Employment and Skills Strategies in Turkey*, OECD Reviews on Local Job Creation, OECD Publishing, Paris.
http://dx.doi.org/10.1787/9789264279506-en

ISBN 978-92-64-27949-0 (print)
ISBN 978-92-64-27950-6 (PDF)
ISBN 978-92-64-27951-3 (epub)

Series: OECD Reviews on Local Job Creation
ISSN 2311-2328 (print)
ISSN 2311-2336 (online)

The statistical data for Israel are supplied by and under the responsibility of the relevant Israeli authorities. The use of such data by the OECD is without prejudice to the status of the Golan Heights, East Jerusalem and Israeli settlements in the West Bank under the terms of international law.

Photo credits: Cover © Andy Dean Photography/Shutterstock.com; © iStockphoto.com/thekopmylife.

Corrigenda to OECD publications may be found on line at: *www.oecd.org/about/publishing/corrigenda.htm*.
© OECD 2017

You can copy, download or print OECD content for your own use, and you can include excerpts from OECD publications, databases and multimedia products in your own documents, presentations, blogs, websites and teaching materials, provided that suitable acknowledgement of OECD as source and copyright owner is given. All requests for public or commercial use and translation rights should be submitted to *rights@oecd.org*. Requests for permission to photocopy portions of this material for public or commercial use shall be addressed directly to the Copyright Clearance Center (CCC) at *info@copyright.com* or the Centre français d'exploitation du droit de copie (CFC) at *contact@cfcopies.com*.

Preface

After years of economic expansion, Turkey's economy faces a number of critical challenges, which could place significant downward pressures on the growth potential of the economy. Unemployment has increased since 2012 and stood at 11.7% in 2016, well above the OECD average. Despite this trend, overall employment has continued to grow. The number of people employed grew by an average annual rate of 3.0% between 2004 and 2013. Turkey is divided into 81 provinces that have strong regional disparities in terms of the distribution of jobs and skills. It is therefore critical to look at the role of local policies in fostering quality job creation, economic development and entrepreneurship opportunities.

Over recent years, the work of the OECD LEED Programme on *Designing Local Skills Strategies, Building Flexibility and Accountability into Local Employment Services, Breaking out of Policy Silos, Leveraging Training and Skills Development in SMEs*, and *Skills for Competitiveness* has demonstrated that local strategies to boost jobs and skills require the participation of many different actors across employment, training, economic development, and social welfare portfolios. Employers, unions and the non-profit sector are also key partners in ensuring that education and training programmes provide the skills needed in the labour markets of today and the future.

The series of *OECD Reviews on Local Job Creation* deliver evidence-based and practical recommendations on how to better support employment and economic development at the local level. This report on Turkey takes a case study approach, analysing the management and implementation of policies in the Turkish provinces of Kocaeli and Trabzon. It provides a comparative framework to understand the role of local labour market policy in matching people to jobs, engaging employers in skills development activities, as well as fostering new growth and economic development opportunities. It includes practical policy examples of actions taken in Turkey to help workers find better quality jobs, while also stimulating productivity and inclusion.

This report shows that going forward, the government should seek opportunities to formalise strategic planning processes within Turkish provinces. Each province should articulate a vision for local employment and economic development, which focuses on strategic growth sectors. This vision should be reinforced by stronger engagement with local employers to ensure that skills development opportunities align with the needs of the world of work. There is also an opportunity to improve the quality of jobs at the local level by introducing workforce development programmes that seek to introduce innovations in how employers use technology in the manufacturing and services sectors.

İŞKUR (the Turkish Employment Agency) should be warmly thanked for their active participation and support of the study.

Foreword

This report was prepared as part of the Local Economic and Employment Development (LEED) Programme within the Centre for Entrepreneurship, SMEs, Local Development, and Tourism (CFE) of the Organisation for Economic Co-operation and Development (OECD). It has been undertaken in co-operation with the Turkish Employment Agency (İŞKUR). Special thanks should be given to Turkish officials within İŞKUR who contributed to this report and participated in the OECD study visits: Askin Toren, Kagan Bayramoglu, Uğur Tunc, and Yasin Velioglu.

Special thanks should also be given to local stakeholders in each of the case study areas of Kocaeli and Trabzon, who participated in meetings and provided documentation and comments critical to the production of the report.

This project is coordinated by Jonathan Barr (Head of the Employment and Skills Unit) who was also one of the principal authors of this report, under the direction of Sylvain Giguère, Head of OECD LEED Division and Lamia Kamal-Chaoui, Director of the Centre for Entrepreneurship, SMEs, Local Development, and Tourism (CFE). The other principal author is Serdar Sayan (TOBB University of Economics and Technology). Michela Meghnagi (OECD), Pierre Georgin (OECD) and Beatriz Jambrina Canseco (OECD) provided valuable statistical and editorial support, which was critical to the production of this report. Randall Eberts, President of the Upjohn Institute for Employment Research in the United States provided valuable advice on the development of this report and participated in the OECD study visit. Thanks also go to François Iglesias and Pauline Arbel for production assistance and Janine Treves who provided useful editorial support.

Table of contents

Executive summary 9

Reader's guide 11

Chapter 1. **Policy context for employment and skills in Turkey** 15
    Economic and labour market trends 16
    Labour market indicators 18
    Level of skills in Turkey 22
    National policy context and policy actions 24
    Notes 32
    References 33

Chapter 2. **Overview of the Turkish case study areas** 35
    Overview 36
    East Marmara – North region and Kocaeli 36
    East Black Sea region and Trabzon 39
    Local labour markets and employment characteristics 42
    Impact of the economic climate and employment policies 43
    Education and training 45
    Mapping skills supply and demand in Turkey 48
    Notes 49
    References 50

Chapter 3. **Local Job Creation Dashboard findings in Turkey** 51
    Overview 52
    Aligning policies and programmes to local economic development . 53
    Flexibility in the delivery of employment and vocational training policies ... 53
    Capacities within employment and VET sectors 57
    Policy co-ordination, policy integration and co-operation with other sectors ... 58
    Evidence based policy making 60
    Adding value through skills 61
    Matching people to jobs and facilitating progression 65
    Integrated local approaches to skills 67
    Targeting policies to local employment sectors and investing in quality jobs ... 67
    Being inclusive 72
    Note 76
    References 77

TABLE OF CONTENTS

Chapter 4. **Towards an action plan for jobs in Turkey: Recommendations and best practices** 79
    Towards an action plan for jobs: Recommendations for Turkey 80
    Better aligning policies and programmes towards local economic development ... 80
    Adding value through skills 83
    Investing in quality jobs and stimulating productivity 85
    Being inclusive 87
    References 90

Tables

  3.1. İŞKUR Career and Job Counselling Services, 2010-14 66
  3.2. Job quality indicators, Turkey ranking and selected averages 69
  3.3. İŞKUR counsellor visits to workplaces, 2010-14 70

Figures

  1.1. GDP Growth rate (%), 2007-15 16
  1.2. Regional GDP per capita (USD PPP, base year 2010, current prices), Turkish TL2 regions, 2011 17
  1.3. Labour force participation rate by sex (15-64 year olds), 2007 and 2015 18
  1.4. Employment rates (total vs. female rates), Turkish regions, 2014 19
  1.5. Employment by industry (% of total employment), Turkey, 2014 20
  1.6. Comparing total unemployment, youth unemployment and long-term unemployment in Turkish regions, 2014 21
  1.7. Unemployment across Turkish provinces, 2013 21
  1.8. Unemployment rate by sex, 2007 and 2015 22
  1.9. Mean literacy and numeracy scores, OECD Survey of Adult Skills (PIAAC), selected OECD countries and OECD average 22
  1.10. Share of tertiary educated adults, Turkey versus OECD, 2015 23
  1.11. Tertiary educational attainment and illiteracy (% of total population), Turkish regions, 2013 24
  1.12. Female tertiary educational attainment vs illiteracy as % of total female population, TL2 regions, 2014 24
  1.13. Turkish Education System 28
  2.1. Provinces of Turkey 36
  2.2. Sectoral composition of employment (%), Eastern Marmara – North region, 2007-15 37
  2.3. Annual value-added per person (USD at current prices), Eastern Marmara-North region and Turkey, 2004-11 38
  2.4. Labour force participation rates, Eastern Marmara – North and Turkey, 2008-13 38
  2.5. Employment rates, Eastern Marmara – North and Turkey, 2008-13 39
  2.6. Unemployment rates, Kocaeli province and Turkey, 2008-13 39
  2.7. Annual value-added per person (USD at current prices), East Black Sea region and Turkey, 2004-11 40
  2.8. Sectoral composition of employment in the East Black Sea region (%), 2007-15 40

2.9. Panel of labour force participation, employment and unemployment rates (respectively), East Black Sea region and Turkey, 2008-13 41
2.10. Working age population (15-64 year old) in Kocaeli and Trabzon, 2007-16 43
2.11. Number of students enrolled in tertiary and higher degree programmes: Kocaeli and Trabzon... 46
2.12. Attendance to capacity ratios for UMEM courses in Kocaeli and Trabzon, 2011-16.. 47
2.13. Understanding the relationship between skills supply and demand 48
2.14. Balancing skills supply and demand in Turkey, 2014 49
3.1. OECD Reviews on Local Job Creation – Dashboard results for Turkey 52
3.2. OECD Dashboard Results for better aligning programmes and policies to local economic development in Turkey 53
3.3. Percentage of PES offices reporting medium to high flexibility in the management of programmes and policies, 2014 55
3.4. Percentage of PES offices reporting more flexibility would be useful in order to respond to local labour market conditions, 2014................ 56
3.5. Adequacy of resources at local PES offices, 2014........................ 58
3.6. Percentage of PES offices conducting specific activities as part of local employment and economic development programmes 59
3.7. OECD Dashboard Results – Adding Value through Skills 61
3.8. OECD Dashboard results – targeting policies to local employment sectors and investing in quality jobs...................................... 67
3.9. Trends in self-employment (%): Turkey and selected OECD countries, 2006-15.. 71
3.10. OECD Dashboard results for being inclusive 72
3.11. Percentage of youth aged 15-29 who are neither employed nor in education or training, 2007 and 2015............................. 75

Follow OECD Publications on:

 http://twitter.com/OECD_Pubs
 http://www.facebook.com/OECDPublications
 http://www.linkedin.com/groups/OECD-Publications-4645871
 http://www.youtube.com/oecdilibrary
 http://www.oecd.org/oecddirect/

Executive summary

Turkey's economy has proved resilient despite a significant number of external threats from the global economy. Future growth is fragile and will depend on improvements in competitiveness and productivity, as well as making better use of existing skills in the economy. Unemployment stood at 11.7% in 2016, which is above the OECD average and contrasts with recent downward trends across many OECD countries. More than 30% of young people in Turkey aged 15-29 were classified as NEET (i.e. not in education, employment or training) in 2014. This value is sharply lower than in 2005, but well above the OECD average of 15.2%.

There is a strong emphasis in Turkey on placing people into jobs. İŞKUR which is the Turkish Public Employment Agency has significantly increased the number of job and vocational counsellors within the employment system to better match job seekers to employers. Provincial Employment and Vocational Training Boards (PEVTBs) across Turkey assist in the process of creating employment policies at the local level and provide suggestions to İŞKUR about the training courses available for unemployed persons. To help Turkey respond to current and future labour market challenges, this OECD report has looked at a range of institutions and bodies involved in employment and skills development policies with a focus on implementation at the local level. Turkey is divided into 81 provinces that have strong regional disparities in terms of employment and economic development opportunities. In-depth work was undertaken in the Turkish provinces of Kocaeli and Trabzon. The province of Kocaeli falls into a high-skills equilibrium while Trabzon is characterised by skills surpluses indicating that greater efforts must be placed on stimulating higher-skill jobs and productivity.

Going forward, stronger efforts must be placed on providing provinces in Turkey with job opportunities that will contribute to their overall economic and social well-being. Building the leadership and governance capacities of local authorities in the implementation of employment and skills policies should be a priority. The following key conclusions and recommendations should be considered.

Key conclusions and recommendations

Better aligning programmes and policies to local economic development

- **Establish local strategic planning processes to integrate employment and economic development efforts:** the government should establish a formal strategic planning process, which would involve stakeholders working together to articulate a vision for the local economy and the priority sectors that need to be developed for future job creation and growth. A small task force in each province could be established to focus on employment and economic development opportunities over the long-term.

- **Develop stronger local research and analytical capacities by leveraging the role of universities in producing labour market information and forecasting skills needs:** local universities should become more engaged in the production of labour market information, which offer insights into the competitive positions of Turkish provinces and sector specific analysis, which could compare the strengths and weaknesses of the local economy.

Adding value through skills

- **Encourage more partnerships between the training system and employers to ensure that skills development programmes are well connected to labour market demand:** employers in Turkey should play a stronger advisory role within the vocational education and training system, advising on course content and service delivery arrangements.

Targeting sectors and investing quality jobs and productivity

- **Foster the better use of talent in the workplace to boost quality job creation and the productive capacities of local economies:** İŞKUR should examine its suite of employment and training programmes to focus on the demand for skills through incentives, which encourage stronger entrepreneurship and skills development opportunities within small and medium-sized enterprises (SMEs).

Being inclusive

- **Launch a youth employment strategy at the national level and identify innovative local approaches, which could be adopted in other regions:** Turkey has one of the highest youth unemployment rates among OECD countries. This includes a large proportion of low-skilled youth. The government should increase access to apprenticeships, internships, and other work-based learning opportunities for youth.
- **Urgently re-focus labour market integration efforts to assist migrants in developing employability skills:** Local governments have a critical role to play in working with migrants to develop concrete and innovative programme responses. In Turkey, the national government can play a facilitating role by working with the provinces to identify "what works" and sharing information among provinces to assist and help migrants build employability skills.

Reader's guide

The OECD Reviews on Local Job Creation involves a series of international comparative reports in Australia, Belgium (Flanders), Canada, Czech Republic, France, Ireland, Israel, Italy (Autonomous Province of Trento), Korea, Poland, Slovenia, Sweden, Turkey, the United Kingdom and the United States (California and Michigan). The key stages of each review are summarised in Box 1.

> **Box 1. Project Methodology for the OECD Reviews on Local Job Creation**
>
> - Analyse available data to understand the key labour market challenges facing the country in the context of the economic recovery and apply an OECD diagnostic tool which seeks to assess the balance between the supply and demand for skills at the local level.
> - Map the current policy framework for employment, skills and economic development policies.
> - Distribute an electronic questionnaire to local labour offices (İŞKUR regional employment offices,) across Turkey to gather information on how they work with other stakeholders to support local job creation policies.
> - Apply the local job creation dashboard in case study areas, developed by the OECD to measure the relative strengths and weaknesses of implementation practices in contributing to job creation.
> - Conduct an OECD study visit, where local and national roundtables with a diverse range of stakeholders are held to discuss the results and refine the findings and recommendations.
> - Contribute to policy development in the reviewed country by proposing policy options to overcome barriers, illustrated by selected good practice initiatives from other OECD countries.

While furthering the recovery from the economic crisis remains a focus for policy-makers, there is a need for both short-term and longer-term actions to ensure sustainable growth. In response to this issue, the OECD LEED Programme has developed a set of thematic areas on which local stakeholders and employment and training agencies can focus efforts. These include:

1. **Better aligning policies and programmes to local economic development challenges and opportunities:** The benefits of better aligning employment, skills and economic development policies are increasingly apparent in the context of the knowledge economy. One of the key advantages that a locality or region can offer a business is the quality of its human capital. In recognition of this, local economic development officials can benefit significantly from working with employment offices and using workforce development as an instrument to attract new firms and stimulate local economic development.

2. **Adding value through skills** by creating an adaptable and capable labour force, and supporting employment progression and skills upgrading;

3. **Targeting policy to local employment sectors and investing in quality jobs**, including gearing education and training to emerging local growth sectors and responding to global trends, while working with employers on skills utilisation and productivity; and,
4. **Being inclusive** to ensure that all actual and potential members of the labour force can contribute to future economic growth.

Local Job Creation Dashboard

Chapter 3 of this report provides a summary of the results of the Local Job Creation dashboard, which is a policy implementation capacity assessment tool developed by the OECD. As part of this international comparative project, the OECD has drawn on its previous research to develop a set of best practice priorities across four thematic areas. The dashboard is used to assess local practice and implementation capacities (see Box 2 for a list of the thematic areas and sub-indicators). A value between 1 (low) to 5 (high) is assigned to each of the indicators corresponding to the relative strengths and weaknesses of local policy approaches based on best practices in other OECD countries. These indicators are established by looking at a range of quantitative and qualitative data at the local level. The dashboard enables national and local policy-makers to gain a clearer overview of the strengths and weaknesses of current policies and programmes, so as to better prioritise future actions and resources.

Box 2. Local Job Creation Dashboard

Better aligning policies and programmes to local economic development
 1.1. Flexibility in the delivery of employment and vocational training policies
 1.2. Capacities within employment and vocational education and training (VET) sectors
 1.3. Policy co-ordination, policy integration and co-operation with other sectors
 1.4. Evidence based policy making

Adding value through skills
 2.1. Flexible training open to all in a broad range of sectors
 2.2. Working with employers on training
 2.3. Matching people to jobs and facilitating progression
 2.4. Joined-up approaches to skills

Targeting policy to local employment sectors and investing in quality jobs
 3.1. Relevance of provision to important local employment sectors and global trends and challenges
 3.2. Working with employers on skills utilisation and productivity
 3.3. Promotion of skills for entrepreneurship
 3.4. Promoting quality jobs through local economic development

Being inclusive
 4.1. Employment and training programmes geared to local "at-risk" groups
 4.2. Childcare and family friendly policies to support women's participation in employment
 4.3. Tackling youth unemployment
 4.4. Openness to immigration

The approach for Turkey

This study has looked at the range of institutions and bodies involved in workforce and skills development in Turkey. In-depth analysis based on document reviews and interviews with key stakeholders was undertaken to look at local employment and economic development activities in two provinces:

- Trabzon
- Kocaeli

In each case study area, interviews were conducted with a wide set of stakeholders. An electronic questionnaire was also sent to managers of İŞKUR regional employment offices in Turkey, which requested information on their management capacities and activities. The questionnaire was administrated during the summer of 2015 and the results are based on 65 responses. In March 2016, local roundtables were held in each of the case study areas and at the national level to discuss the findings and recommendations. These meetings brought together a range of stakeholders, including relevant department officials in the fields of employment, economic development, and training; employers; and other local community and social development organisations.

References

Froy, F., S. Giguère and E. Travkina (2010), *Local Job Creation: Project Methodology*, OECD Local Economic and Employment Development (LEED), OECD, Paris, *www.oecd.org/cfe/leed/Local%20Job%20Creation%20 Methodology_27%20February.pdf*.

Chapter 1

Policy context for employment and skills in Turkey

> *This chapter provides an overview of the employment and skills system in Turkey. The chapter also provides a description of the main government department actors at the national level in Turkey. Following the global financial crisis, Turkey's economy has shown favourable signs of robustness but a number of significant labour market challenges may hold back its growth potential. These include strong disparities across regions on education and employment outcomes as well as gender gaps in wages and labour force participation.*

Economic and labour market trends

As with other OECD countries, the financial crisis in 2009 had an unfavourable economic impact on Turkey; however, the economy has rebounded in subsequent years and shows favourable signs of robustness. Turkey's strong growth over the past decade has paved the way for convergence in living standards with higher-income OECD countries (OECD, 2016a). Following a strong recovery in 2010 and 2011, the Turkish economy grew at an average annual rate of 6.1% between 2012 and 2015 (see Figure 1.1).

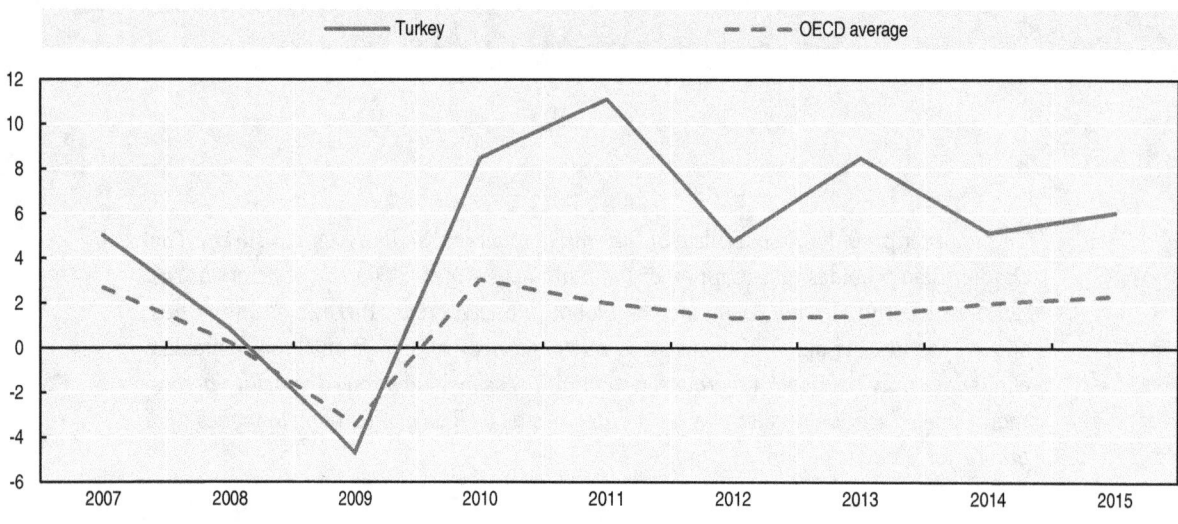

Figure 1.1. **GDP Growth rate (%), 2007-15**

Source: OECD (2016b).

Despite enjoying rapid growth following the economic crisis, the Turkish economy is having a difficult time generating quality employment opportunities for all members of the labour market. While employment rates consistently rose during and after the crisis, 43.9% of all 15-64 year olds were still outside of the labour force in 2015 (Turkstat, 2016a). This is in part due to widespread participation in the informal economy, which amounted to 30.6% of the Turkish labour force in 2009 (ILO, 2012).

Furthermore, there remain significant gaps between Turkey and other OECD countries on a number of key economic and social indicators. At USD 24 000 in 2016 (constant prices, 2010 PPP), Turkey's GDP per capita was the fourth lowest among OECD countries. While absolute poverty, measured as the share of people living below the national poverty line, dropped between 2006 and 2014 from 13.3% to 1.6%, relative poverty has increased; 15% of the Turkish population earned less than 50% of the median income in 2014, compared to an OECD average of 11%. This is in spite of workers putting in very long hours; Turkish employees in the formal economy work an average of 47.7 hours per week, compared to a European Union average of 37.4 hours (Eurostat, 2015). In addition, gender gaps between men and women in wage levels and labour force participation are more pronounced than in other OECD countries (OECD, 2016a).

Turkey also has strong disparities across its regions on a number of key economic and labour market indicators. One can see strong regional variations in GDP per capita (see Figure 1.2) and disposable income levels. In 2011, income was highest in Istanbul, at almost USD 27 000 per capita, with Ankara and Izmir showing similarly high rates. GDP per capita was lowest in the Eastern, North-eastern and South-eastern Anatolian regions of the country, all of which featured figures ranging from USD 7 000-13 000 (OECD, 2013). As a result of their relatively lower economic performance, these were also the provinces with the highest net internal migration outflows.

Figure 1.2. **Regional GDP per capita (USD PPP, base year 2010, current prices), Turkish TL2 regions, 2011**

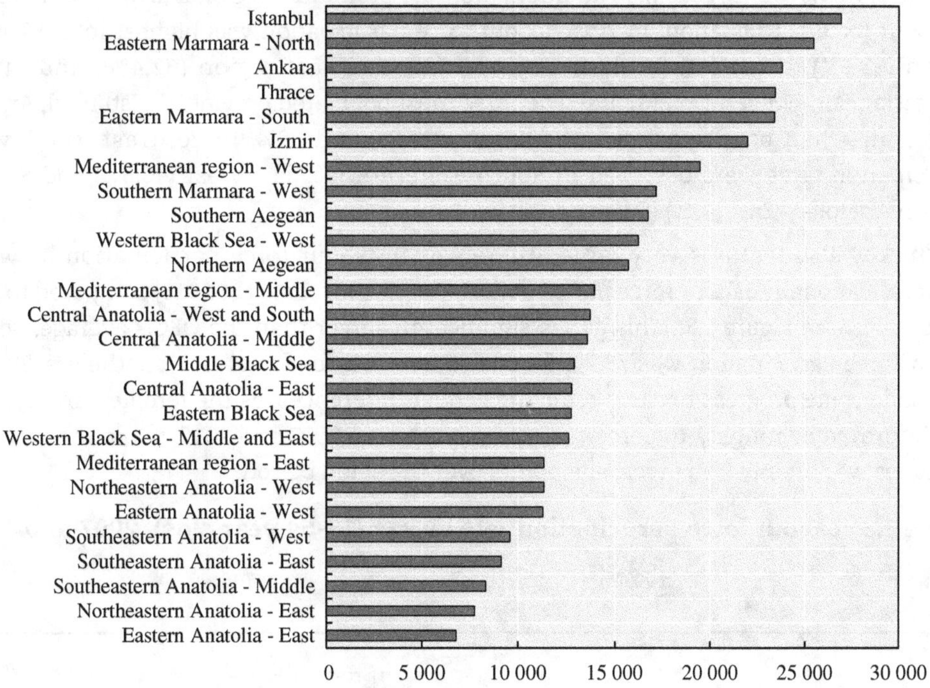

Source: OECD (2012).

In response, the government has launched a series of programmes that are designed to reduce disparities between regions, including a comprehensive incentive structure involving tax cuts, tax breaks and write-offs designed to promote investment and employment generation in relatively less developed regions. In addition to these incentives, overseen primarily by the Ministry of Economy, there are various programmes supported by regional development agencies, such as the Regional Competitiveness Operational Programme run by the Ministry of Science, Industry and Technology. These programmes are partly funded through the European Union (EU)'s Instrument for Pre-Accession Assistance (IPA) and they focus both on increasing the competitiveness of the Turkish economy and supporting its convergence with those of EU countries as well as on reducing regional socio-economic disparities. The programme includes support for transition and institution building, regional and cross-border co-operation, and regional, rural and human resources development. It focuses on the 43 provinces where income per capita is 75% below the Turkish national average.

Labour market indicators

In spite of high growth and significant improvements in its labour market performance in recent years, Turkey faces important challenges in the form of large regional and gender gaps in labour outcomes as well as limited participation in the formal economy. Indeed, evidence suggests that there is a high presence of informal employment throughout Turkey. According to the International Labour Organization (ILO), nearly 5 million people (3.7 million men and 1.1 million women) were in informal occupations in Turkey in 2009. Informal employment is especially high in the construction sector, where 55% of all individuals employed worked informally in 2009 (ILO, 2012).

Weak participation in the formal economy is reflected in the labour force participation rate (i.e. the share of people aged 15-64 that are economically active). Even though it increased from 49.8% in 2006 to 56.1% in 2015, the figure remains well below the OECD average of 71.3% (OECD, 2016a). In addition, there are prominent regional disparities in terms of labour force participation. In 2015, labour force participation was highest in the Thrace region (63.9%), the Western Black Sea – Middle and East region (62.4%), and in the Mediterranean – West region (61.1%). The three most populated provinces – Istanbul, Ankara and Izmir – had participation rates between 56% and 60%. In contrast, the lowest participation rates were observed in South-eastern Anatolia – West (46.6%) and South-eastern Anatolia – East (41%) (Eurostat, 2015).

Turkey also features very large differences in labour force participation between genders. Nationally, labour force participation was 77% for males in 2015, compared to 35% for females (see Figure 1.3). This gap is significantly larger than the OECD average, where labour force participation was 79.7% for males and 63% for females. Nonetheless, Turkey has made some progress towards reducing gender differences, as the female participation rate improved by roughly 10 percentage points between 2007 and 2015, while the increase for males was of only 2.6 percentage points over the same period.

Figure 1.3. **Labour force participation rate by sex (15-64 year olds), 2007 and 2015**

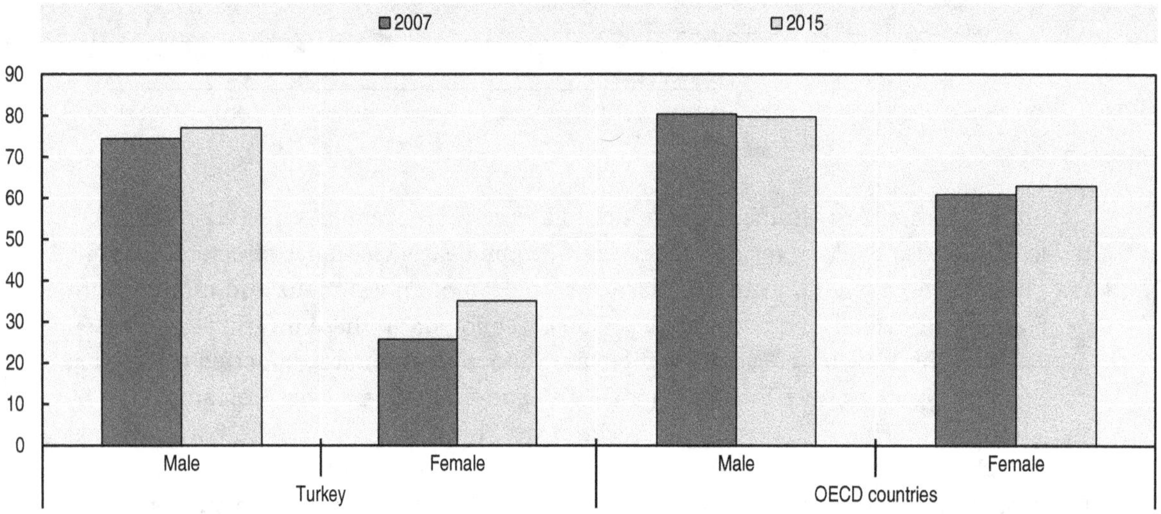

Source: OECD (2016d).

Employment rates in Turkey show signs of improvement, although further advances will be necessary to attain convergence with other OECD countries. While average annual employment growth reached 4% between 2009 and 2014, only half of the working age population (15-64 year olds) was employed in 2014 (OECD, 2016a). This rate was 16 percentage points lower than the OECD average of 66%, but 5 percentage points higher than in 2007 (OECD, 2016a).

Similarly to labour force participation figures, significant disparities exist across Turkish regions in terms of employment rates. In 2014, employment rates were highest in the Western Black Sea – Middle and East region (58%) and in North-eastern Anatolia – East (57%) (see Figure 1.4). On the other hand, they were lowest in the East and Middle areas of South-eastern Anatolia at 30% and 37% respectively (OECD, 2016e).

Gender gaps are also large. On average, female employment rates amount to just two-thirds of the total employment rate, but the difference can be even greater in less-developed regions. For example, in the eastern part of South-eastern Anatolia, the female employment rate is merely 11% in comparison to the overall rate of 30%.

Figure 1.4. **Employment rates (total vs. female rates), Turkish regions, 2014**

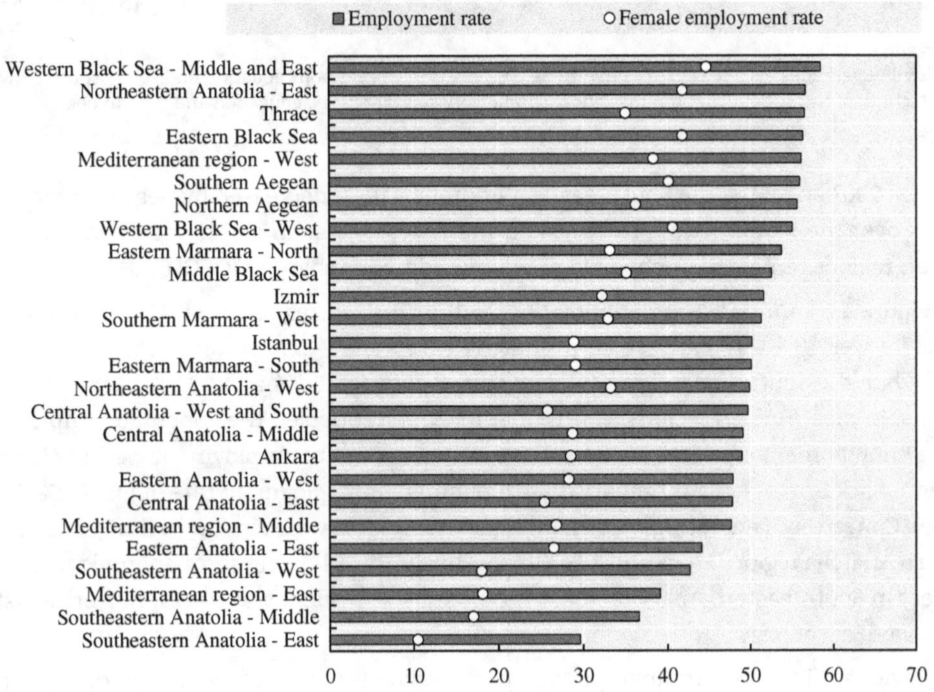

Source: OECD (2016e).

When looking at employment distribution by sector in Turkey in 2014 (see Figure 1.5), the largest share of total employment was within the distributive trade, repairs, transport, accommodation and food service activities sector (23%). The share of employment in agriculture, forestry and fishing (21%) was also high, particularly in comparison to other OECD countries. Public administration and other public employment occupied 14% of the total (OECD, 2016e).

With regards to unemployment, the national rate fluctuated around 10% over the period between 2007 and 2014, with the exception of 2009 when it reached 14%. In comparison, the OECD average increased from 5.8% to 7.6% within the same period (OECD, 2016b). Nonetheless, patterns over time diverged across the different Turkish regions. For instance, while the unemployment rate in the sub-region of Izmir increased by 4.5 percentage points

Figure 1.5. **Employment by industry (% of total employment), Turkey, 2014**

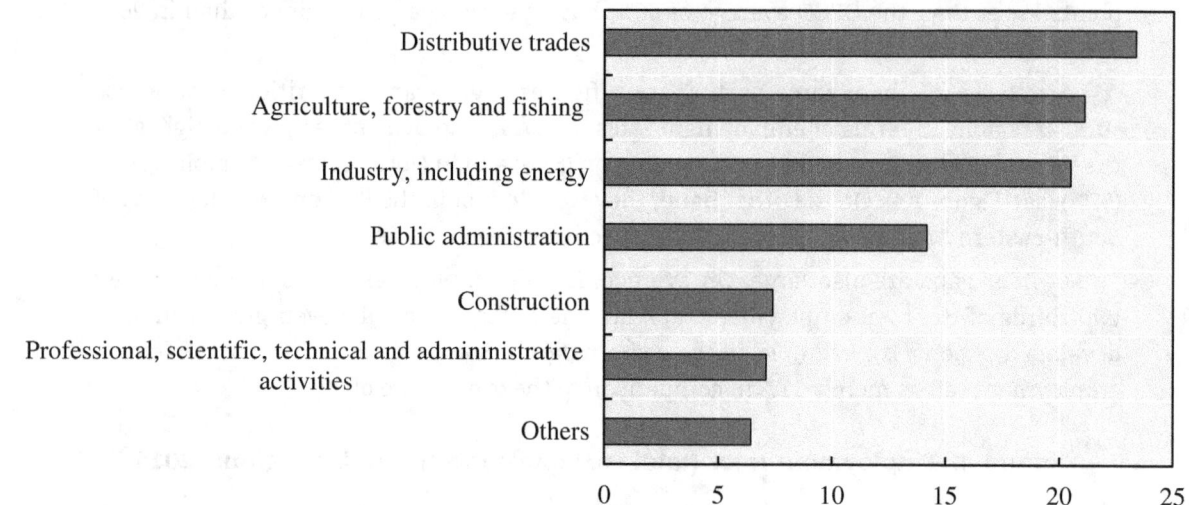

1. All categories add up to 100.
2. The label "distributive trades" includes distributive trade, repairs, transport, accommodation and food service activities. The label "public administration" includes public administration, compulsory social security, education and human health.

Source: OECD (2016c).

between 2007 and 2014, the South-eastern Anatolia – West decreased by nearly 9 percentage points over the same period. In contrast, many regions such as Thrace or the Northern Aegean regions remained unchanged or witnessed minor changes (OECD, 2016e).

Figure 1.6 summarises unemployment within Turkish regions in 2014. Unemployment varied between 3.4% in South-eastern Anatolia – East and 24.1% in North-eastern Anatolia – East, while the youth unemployment rate varied between 5.9% and 33.2% in the same two regions. In most Turkish regions, youth unemployment doubled the general unemployment rate, although there are some outliers. For example, youth unemployment was 18.4% in the Eastern Black Sea region, in comparison to a national unemployment rate of just 6.2% (OECD, 2016e). Conversely, general and youth unemployment rates were similar in the Middle South-eastern Anatolia region (17.5% and 19.4% respectively). In 2014, long-term unemployment was highest in South-eastern Anatolia – East region at 5.7%, while it was lowest in North-eastern Anatolia – East at 0.3%.

Regional disparities in unemployment can be better understood when looking at the provincial level map of Turkey. Figure 1.7 shows the unemployment trends across Turkey's provinces in 2013. Most provinces' figures were lower than 10%: 35 provinces had a rate of less than 7%, while the remaining 25 had rates between 7-10%. 14 provinces were in the medium-high range between 10-15%, including the provinces of Ankara and Istanbul, while 7 provinces had an unemployment rate higher than 15%, including Izmir with 15.4% (Turkstat, 2016a).

Considering unemployment rates by gender (see Figure 1.8), the gap between male and female figures in Turkey is significantly higher than the OECD average. In 2015, 12.9% of female aged 15-64 were unemployed, an increase of over one percentage point since 2007. Unemployment among males decreased in the same period by less than one percentage point to reach 9.4% in 2014. The OECD average was close to 7% both for males and females in the same year (OECD, 2016d).

The NEET rate (share of youth that are not in employment, education or training), which stands at around 35% at the national level, is the highest among OECD countries, and shows

Figure 1.6. **Comparing total unemployment, youth unemployment and long-term unemployment in Turkish regions, 2014**

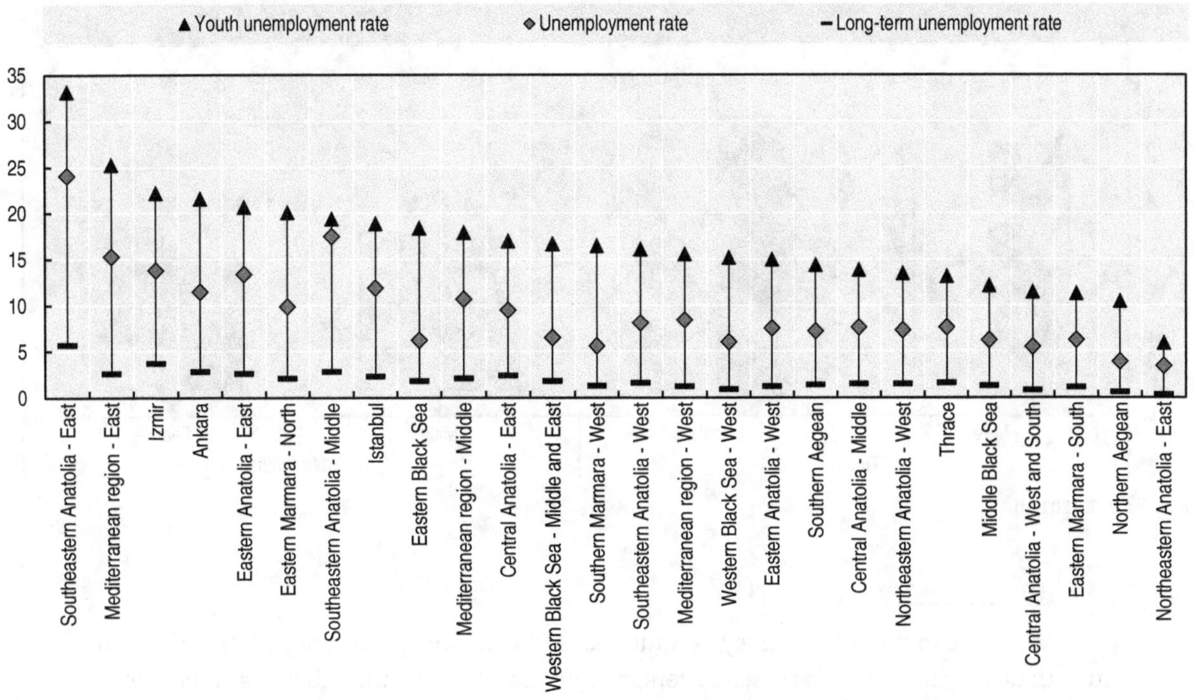

▲ Youth unemployment rate   ◆ Unemployment rate   — Long-term unemployment rate

Source: OECD (2016e).

Figure 1.7. **Unemployment across Turkish provinces, 2013**

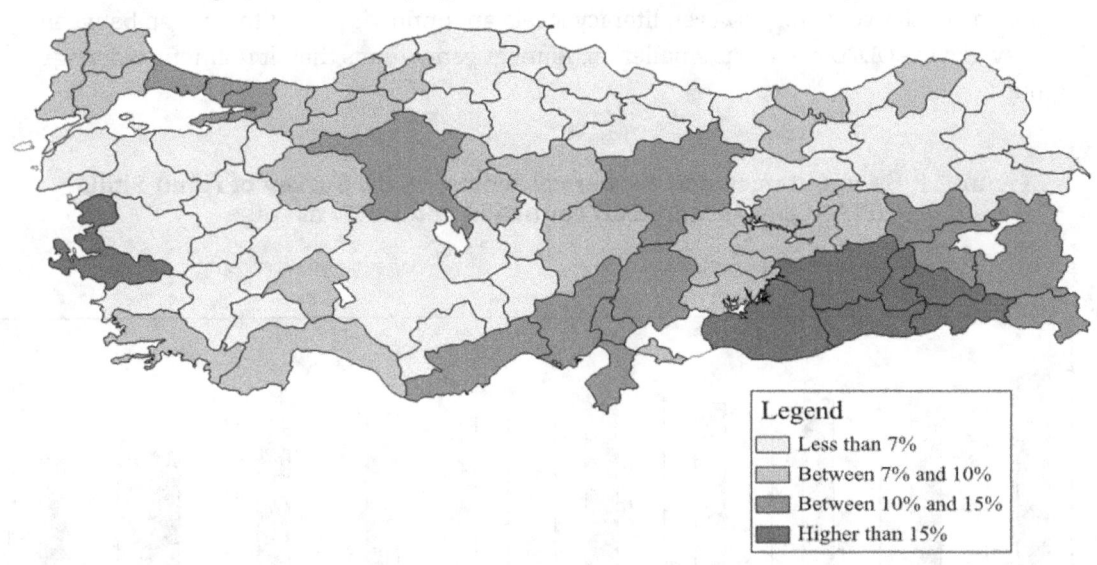

Legend
- Less than 7%
- Between 7% and 10%
- Between 10% and 15%
- Higher than 15%

Source: Turkstat (2016a).

an average gender gap of about 30 percentage points (OECD, 2013 and 2015).[1] Part of the reason underlying the high NEET rate is the mismatch between skills demanded by employers and those acquired by the workforce. Nonetheless, Turkey has seen important improvements in this regard over the past years: its NEET rate saw the second sharpest decline among all OECD countries between 2005 and 2014 (OECD, 2015).

Figure 1.8. **Unemployment rate by sex, 2007 and 2015**

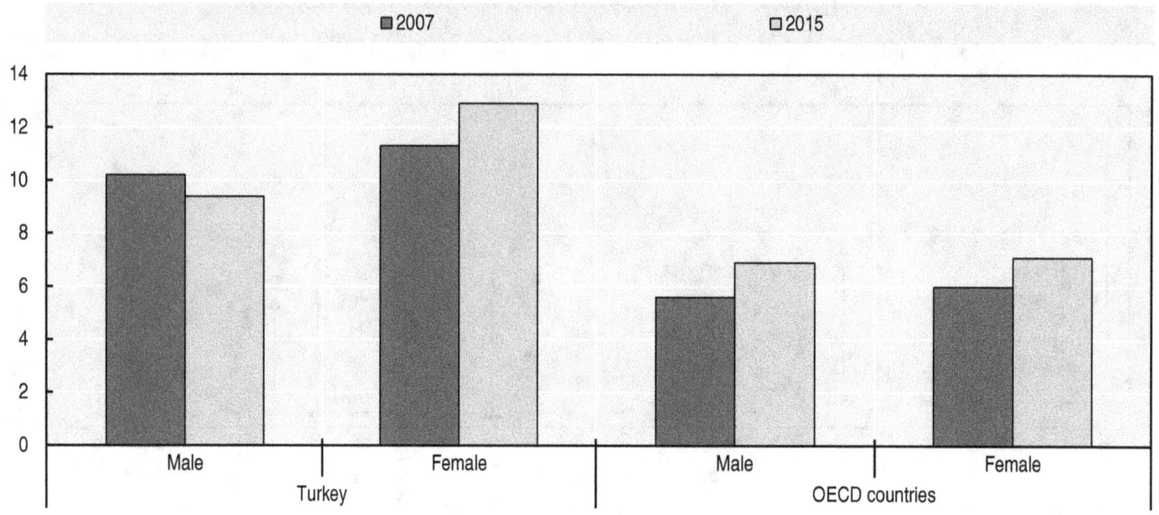

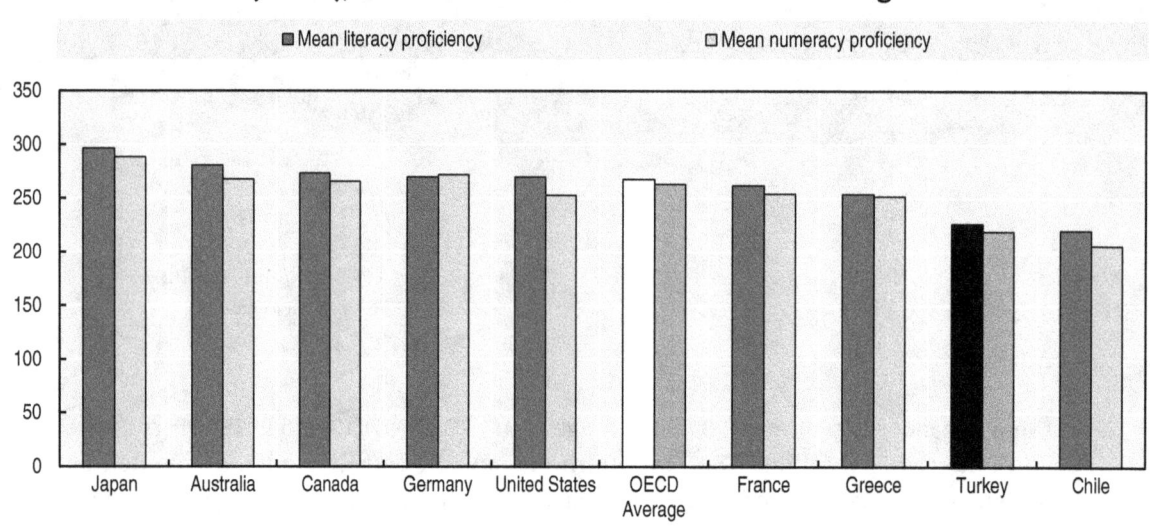

Source: OECD (2016d).

Level of skills in Turkey

According to the OECD Survey of Adult Skills (PIAAC), the proficiency of Turkish adults in both literacy and numeracy is, on average, significantly lower than that of adults in other OECD countries, with the exception of Chile (see Figure 1.9). In addition, they show limited proficiency, on average, in problem solving in technology-rich environments (OECD, 2016g). These results reflect the fact that educational attainment among the Turkish population tends to be relatively low. However, literacy levels are improving: the literacy gap between Turkey and the OECD average is smaller for younger generations than it is among older age groups.

Figure 1.9. **Mean literacy and numeracy scores, OECD Survey of Adult Skills (PIAAC), selected OECD countries and OECD average**

Source: OECD (2017a).

A significant gender gap can be observed in Turkey in terms of the proficiency in information-processing skills, with men scoring higher than women in all of the three domains assessed (OECD, 2016g). This gender difference, which is particularly pronounced among older adults, reflects the fact that Turkish women tend to have lower educational attainment than men. Nevertheless, contrary to most other OECD countries, higher educational attainment or skills proficiency are not necessarily associated with better employment outcomes, although there is a strong impact of education on wage levels (OECD, 2016g).

In terms of tertiary educational attainment, Turkey performs worse than the average OECD country: 18% of the adult population in Turkey has a tertiary degree compared to an OECD average of 35%. The differences are particularly large as regards the percentage of adults with Bachelor's and Master's degrees (see Figure 1.10)

Figure 1.10. **Share of tertiary educated adults, Turkey versus OECD, 2015**

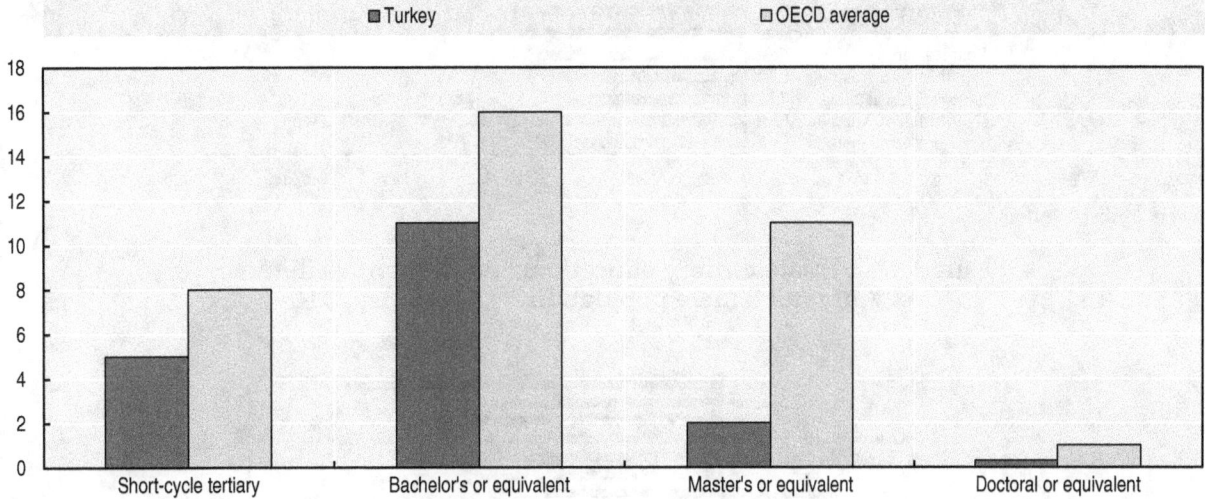

Source: OECD (2017b).

However, these gaps in educational attainment are not as pronounced in Turkey's most important cities. In 2014, the highest share of people with tertiary education was found in the Western part of the country and in the three most populated regions in Turkey: the capital city Ankara (20%), Izmir (16%) and Istanbul (16%) (see Figure 1.11). Tertiary educational attainment was lowest in the Eastern parts of Anatolia (around 8%). Female tertiary education rates show similar trends, albeit with slightly lower values than for the total population (see Figure 1.12).

The level of illiteracy is still a pressing concern in Turkey. In several regions, the share of illiterate people nears the percentage of people with tertiary education – and, in Southeastern Anatolia – East and Middle, Northeastern Anatolia – East, and Eastern Anatolia – East, it even exceeds it. Female illiteracy rates are significantly higher than average, and reach around 20% of the total female population in the previously mentioned regions.

Figure 1.11. **Tertiary educational attainment and illiteracy (% of total population), Turkish regions, 2013**

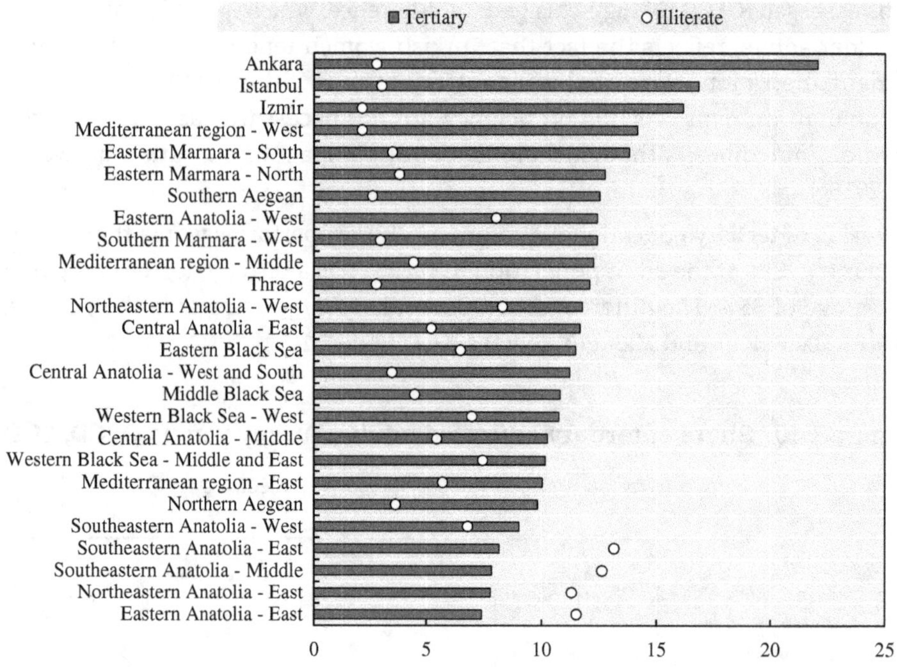

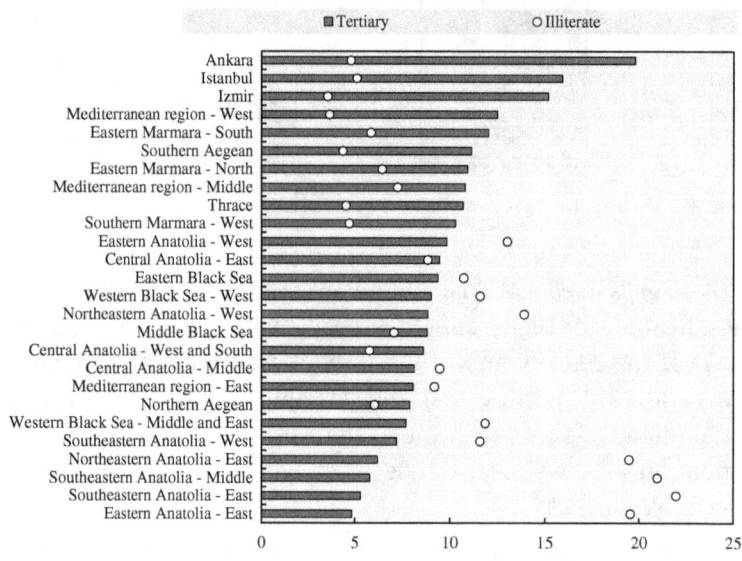

Source: Turkstat (2016b).

Figure 1.12. **Female tertiary educational attainment vs illiteracy as % of total female population, TL2 regions, 2014**

Source: Turkstat (2016b).

National policy context and policy actions

To address the country's labour market and skills challenges, the Turkish Government initiated a series of reforms and long-term commitments as set out in various laws, strategic documents, action plans and programmes, all of which have recognised the critical importance of employment and skills policies. For example, the *Strengthening Vocational and Technical Education and Training (SVET)* project, conducted between 2002 and 2007, aimed to address "the mismatch between education/training programmes and the needs of the labour market," starting with a review of existing practices and policies which paved the way to set new standards for vocational education and training (VET). Launched for the same purpose, the *Modernisation of Vocational Education and Training (MVET)* project included initiatives "to improve VET teacher quality, such as the introduction of VET teacher competencies and quality assurance based on the European Network System" (World Bank, 2014).

In parallel, efforts have been undertaken to align employment and skills policies at the local level. An early step in that direction came in 2002 when the Ministry of National Education (MoNE) issued a regulation to facilitate the creation of a suitable environment for better vocational and technical education across Turkey. The regulation stipulated that the "Provincial Boards of Vocational Education" (PVEBs – or IMEKs) scattered across Turkey would serve as platforms for stakeholder engagement. While this represented a step in the right direction to create a more labour market-friendly vocational education system, the need for complementary action was evident.

Many of these actions required collaboration between different ministries and agencies, as well as co-operation from stakeholders. To co-ordinate such collaboration and co-operation at the local level, *Provincial Boards of Vocational Education* (IMEKs) were converted into *Provincial Boards of Employment and Vocational Education* (PEVTBs or IIMEKs) in 2006. This reform required that the provincial network of the Turkish Public Employment Service (PES – or İŞKUR) join forces with PVEBs to create a larger stakeholder platform with the aim of identifying local courses of action and finding the right balance between demands of employers and capabilities of the central government in each province.

Founded by Law No. 4904, İŞKUR is the primary agency in charge of reducing unemployment and facilitating better matches between supply and demand in the labour market. It is a financially and administratively autonomous public entity operating under the auspices of the Ministry of Labour and Social Security. Its operations are subject to civil law. İŞKUR is comprised of a General Board, the Executive Board and the General Directorate. PEVTBs are considered bodies that are accountable to İŞKUR. Provincial İŞKUR directors report to the General Directorate in Ankara.

Active labour market programmes (ALMP) were limited until İŞKUR was established (ILO, 2003). During the 2000s, the focus of labour market policies has gradually shifted away from the protection of jobs towards active labour market programmes (World Bank, 2006). The number of unemployed people that benefited from employment support services such as vocational training has expanded significantly between 2008 (30 000 trainees) and 2012 (464 000 trainees, representing around 20% of the registered unemployed) (World Bank, 2013).

İŞKUR itself has expanded considerably in recent years: its staff almost doubled and its budget was raised sufficiently to allow for a five-fold increase in resources allocated to active labour market programmes. In addition to provincial offices, İŞKUR has 73 service centres scattered across Turkey. İŞKUR currently employs about 600 full time staff in the General Directorate and about 7 500 full time staff in provincial offices and local service centres (İŞKUR, 2015).

The General Board of İŞKUR is an advisory board that is expected to contribute to the development of employment policies and make suggestions to the General Directorate based on their assessment of progress towards various labour market policy goals. The Executive Board manages the "Unemployment Insurance Fund", decides on the agency's budget and approves contracts involving spending above USD 150 000. It also discusses various operational and policy proposals made by the General Director or members of the Executive Board.

The General Directorate runs İŞKUR and its provincial network, including local service centres. The creation of PEVTBs in 2008 significantly increased the effectiveness and outreach of İŞKUR at the local level. PEVTBs serve not just as a platform for stakeholder engagement in the area of employment but also in vocational training and lifelong learning. Opportunities for continuing education and training for all groups, including workers, jobseekers and disadvantaged individuals, are created and implemented through collaboration between different stakeholders under the PEVTB umbrella. Financing from national sources and EU funds are used to implement joint skills development initiatives and effective matching schemes, based on better labour market information and the identification of employers' needs.

New procedures and tools were introduced to better understand the dynamics of local labour markets and measure the magnitude of demand for various types of skills. Active labour market policies (ALMP) with a strong focus on upgrading skills (training, entrepreneurship, on-the-job training and placement) were adopted and made increasingly sensitive to the needs of particular groups. İŞKUR's capacity to provide career counselling and guidance has also been significantly improved, thanks to greater co-operation with schools, municipalities, the private sector and other stakeholders, as well as the expansion of its human resources. More than 4 000 job and vocational counsellors have been hired and are expected to stay in continuous touch with local employers while providing counselling and guidance to local jobseekers.

> **Box 1.1. Provincial Boards of Employment and Vocational Education (PEVTBs)**
>
> PEVTBs are important instruments of social dialogue and local inter-institutional collaboration that produce solutions for local problems by mobilising local facilities and resources to tackle unemployment and skills gaps. This includes identifying, monitoring and formulating training solutions to meet the skills needs of local labour markets and to prevent employment losses.
>
> PEVTBs meet quarterly to decide on employment policies and strategies and prepare local action plans and monitor their implementation. A sub-committee produces the action plans for the implementation of the decisions taken and determines the party (or parties) in charge. Secretariat duties are carried out jointly by the Provincial İŞKUR Directorate and the Provincial Directorate of the Ministry of National Education. The Executive Committee follows up on the decisions taken and surveys the local labour market.
>
> These local boards enable partnerships with the private sector in assessing and meeting VET needs in general and in the context of active labour market programmes developed to improve skill levels of different groups (workers, jobseekers, disadvantaged individuals). No formal assessment or evaluation of PEVTBs performance has been carried out.

Management of vocational education and training policies

The issue of access to VET programmes arises from the need to accommodate a young population that continues to increase relatively rapidly, but also from regional disparities. The 10th Development Plan of Turkey (Ministry of Development, 2014a) for instance, explicitly refers to the need to broaden the access to VET programmes in light of disparities in regional development.[2] Having a more accessible VET system is a precondition for Turkish firms to move up the value chain, benefit from productivity gains, and thus be more competitive in international markets. It is also crucial for providing individuals with career opportunities, creating quality jobs, and thus moving towards a more inclusive economic model.

In Turkey, various educational degrees (or diplomas) and training programmes are offered by public and private sector organisations (including NGOs) in order for individuals to acquire the skills needed by the labour market, generate employment and promote social inclusion. The structure of the education system in Turkey offers a choice between vocational and general education at secondary and tertiary levels, following the completion of primary education (which was recently set to last four years) and lower-secondary or middle school education. The vocational education offered at the upper-secondary and university level can be complemented with a variety of training programmes, which range from in-company on-the-job training programmes to training courses for the un(der)employed or for individuals who simply wish to acquire new skills.

The national authorities in charge of education, training, employment, social inclusion, science and technology, and regional development, as well as universities and research institutes, training providers, chambers and employers' associations, trade unions, municipalities, and NGOs make up the actors of the vocational education and training (VET) system. These actors work together to identify the ways and means of making the whole VET system more responsive to the medium- to long-term human resource needs of the country and local labour markets, while improving competitiveness as well as social inclusion.

The VET system in Turkey is made up of two types of institutional actors: those that offer educational degree programmes (leading to a diploma) and those that offer training courses (that may or may not lead to a nationally recognised certificate of completion). The major actors offering degree programmes are: 1) vocational high schools at the upper-secondary level (grades 9th through 12th) and apprenticeship schools, and 2) vocational schools at the tertiary level that offer 2-year or 4-year post-secondary degrees (see Figure 1.13).[3] In both cases, programmes offered by private institutions contribute to or complement publicly provided VET schemes.

The Ministry of National Education (MoNE) is the chief institution responsible for co-ordinating VET education at the *upper-secondary* level, including apprenticeship programmes. The Basic Law of National Education puts the MoNE in charge of the whole education system except for the tertiary level. In line with Turkey's centralised public administration system, the ministry hires and appoints teachers and other personnel working at public schools, funds the schools, and decides on the curricula and approves textbooks. At the national level, General Directorates in charge of different levels or types of education, such as pre-school education, primary education, secondary education and vocational education, are responsible for ensuring that all education activities are in compliance with the relevant laws, regulations and policies. The ministry also has a local area network made up of Provincial Directorates which oversee the day-to-day conduct of schools in the 81 provinces and their districts across the country.

The same rules apply to private high schools that offer vocational education diplomas. These have to be accredited by the Ministry of National Education (MoNE) and follow ministry-approved curricula. In addition to vocational high schools that are run for profit, there is a noteworthy public-private partnership (PPP) initiative in vocational education at the secondary level. Recent legislation allows Organised Industrial Zone (OIZ) administrations that build and run vocational high schools within the OIZ to receive funding from the

Figure 1.13. **Turkish Education System**

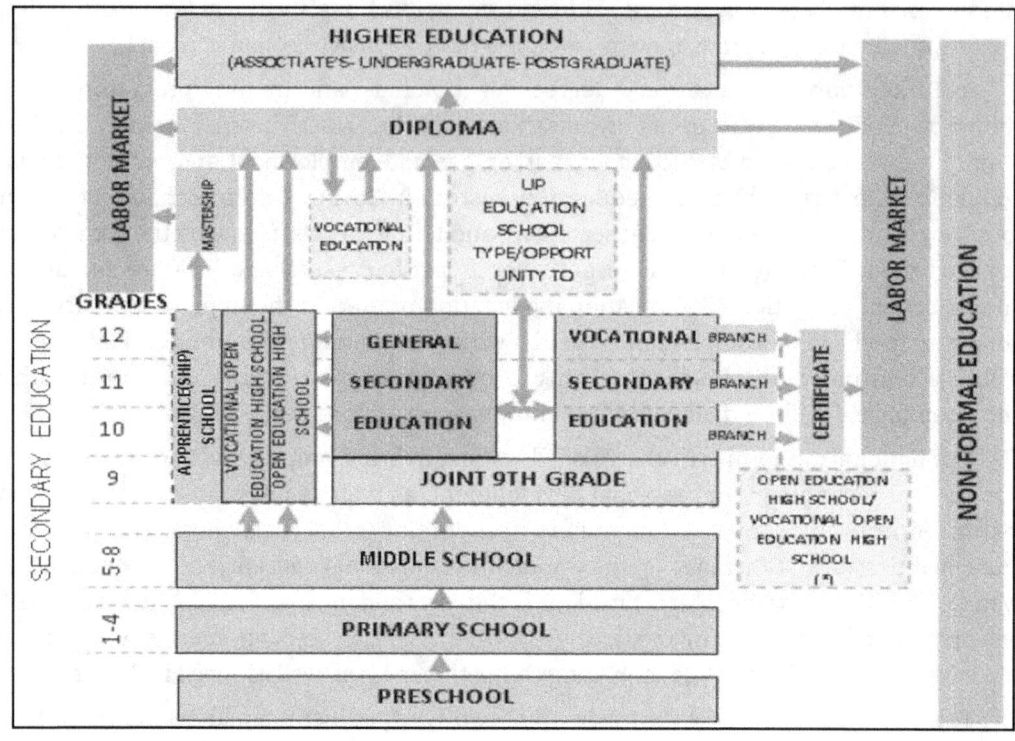

Source: Turkey's VET Strategy: 2014-2018.

government for each student enrolled in the school. The amount of funding paid per student varies depending on the field of concentration, and can be as high as 150% of the average cost to the state of each student enrolled in a public vocational high school. The curriculum to be followed at these schools is jointly prepared by teachers, academics and sector representatives based on workforce needs analysis, professional standards and national competencies, and approved by the MoNE.

Vocational (or "Applied") schools at the tertiary level are attended by graduates of high schools who seek two-year or four-year degrees. These schools of tertiary education operate as part of a university and offer their degrees under the seal of that university. For almost all practical purposes, a degree obtained from a four-year vocational school attended after high school is seen as equivalent to a regular university degree, as it is accredited by the Council of Higher Education, the institution that oversees all universities in Turkey (public and private[4]). Degrees from two-year applied schools attended after high school are treated as associate degrees.

Non-degree training programmes, on the other hand, are offered by a wider spectrum of actors ranging from the Ministry of National Education, which operates a large network of adult (or continuous) education centres scattered around Turkey, to training courses offered by private companies or non-profit foundations, municipalities, chambers and employers' associations or other NGOs.

Concerning the training programmes provided by the public sector, Ministry of National Education's nationwide network of "Public Education Centres" is overseen by the General Directorate for Life-Long Learning and provides continuing vocational training for adults as well as other skills-enhancing courses. İŞKUR also conducts training programmes as part of its suite of active labour market programmes. Offered in two categories to promote the acquisition or enhancement of skills and entrepreneurship, these programmes differ from formal vocational education in terms of the diversity of age groups and education levels, and often target the unemployed. The broader goal of the training courses provided by İŞKUR is to integrate various segments of the population into the labour market and to increase labour market participation. Some of the training courses present employment guarantees in the case of successful completion. Municipalities are also among the public providers of training courses that promote skills enhancement and entrepreneurship.

Within the private sector, for-profit institutions offering VET courses by charging a tuition fee must be registered and accredited by the Ministry of National Education. Similarly, İŞKUR purchases the delivery of many of the training courses that follow pre-approved curricula from sub-contractors or companies. Free or subsidised vocational training or skill-enhancing programmes are also offered by non-profit foundations, chambers and employers' associations and other NGOs, often through social responsibility initiatives. Some of these initiatives, however, are not co-ordinated and offer training based on non-standard curricula, sometimes taught by unaccredited trainers.

There are also examples of co-operation between private sector or non-profits and the public sector in the provision of vocational training courses for such purposes as reducing skill shortages, combatting unemployment, or facilitating the integration of young people, women and disadvantaged groups into the labour market. Such public-private partnerships enable people to acquire and supply the skills most needed in the labour market, thus reducing unemployment and promoting social inclusion (ETF, 2015). Notable examples include social responsibility initiatives backed by large industrial groups such as the Koç Group or Elginkan Group, various sectoral initiatives – or initiatives involving the local chambers – such as the BUTGEM project or ÖZİMEK project, and the UMEM project involving the Turkish Union of the Chambers and Exchanges (TOBB).

Among these initiatives, the Koç Group (the largest industrial group in Turkey) has launched a programme in co-operation with the Ministry of National Education that aims to increase the popularity of vocational high schools among young and successful students by offering scholarships and providing mentorship and guidance, as well as attractive internship and career opportunities.[5] The initiative also supports awareness-raising activities to promote vocational high schools and funds infrastructure improvement projects at public vocational schools. The Elginkan Group's social responsibility initiative is funded by the affiliated Foundation, which runs technical and vocational training centres in three different cities (Bolu, İzmit and Manisa), where a wide range of ministry-certified courses are taught by public vocational school teachers and instructors.

A similar initiative is the non-profit training centre, BUTGEM, funded and run by the Bursa Chamber of Commerce and Industry. Like Elginkan, BUTGEM offers a wide range of technical and vocational training courses in collaboration with the Ministry of National Education without charging the trainees. Other initiatives involving a local chamber include training courses offered within the framework of the ÖZİMEK project carried out in İstanbul jointly by the Gubernatorial Fund Administration and the Chamber of Commerce, in collaboration with the local İŞKUR and Ministry of National Education branches. More than 5 000 people were trained annually during the nearly six years this programme was implemented. Besides these diversified training programmes above, there are initiatives with a sectoral focus such as the one taken by Sütaş, one of the largest dairy companies in Turkey.[6]

Perhaps the most notable and systematic of all these co-operative schemes is the UMEM (or "Skills '10") project that is being carried out nationally by a joint public-private consortium made up of TOBB, İŞKUR, the Ministry of Labour and Social Security and the Ministry of National Education. When the UMEM (or Specialised Occupational Development Centres) project was first introduced in 2010, there were about 2.7 million unemployed in the country but many manufacturing job openings posted by employers were staying unfilled because jobseekers did not have the necessary skills. The project aimed to reduce the severity of these skills shortages by allowing the unemployed to acquire such skills through training courses offered in selected public vocational high schools outside regular class hours. Infrastructure and educational facilities at these schools were considerably improved through an initial investment of about USD 100 million.

Unemployed people registered with İŞKUR could enrol in these courses, which also covered certain service industry jobs free of charge. Individuals received a pre-determined amount for their per diem expenses and are provided health and accident insurance coverage during the training period. The project was funded by İŞKUR and ended on 8 May 2016. The programme combined both theoretical, in-class training, and workplace training – typically at plants or establishments with reported skills shortages, which allowed them to be seriously considered for employment at the same company. If a trainee was employed after successful completion of both the in-class and workplace components of the training, the company that employs her/him received tax and social security benefits (which lasted longer if the trainee employed was younger than 29 or a woman). Within the scope of UMEM, 225 000 people were trained and approximately 75% of them were employed.

Provincial Course Management Boards have been established by the UMEM project, which included the Provincial Directors of İŞKUR and the MoNE, along with principals of vocational high schools that served as project training centres in the province, and the secretary general of the local chamber of industry, who was typically the chairperson of the board. Demand for workers with the skills most needed by local employers was collected through the local chamber, and the board quickly decided which training courses to open based on this information. The UMEM Provincial Course Management Boards have generally been more flexible than PEVTBs and have managed to overcome many bureaucratic obstacles, with the help and support of the national Executive Committee for the project. They have also contributed to the development of "a culture of institutional collaboration that can form the backbone of integrated inclusive growth policies at regional and local levels" (ETF, 2015: 35).

Building on the experience of the UMEM project, the Vocational Training and Employment Mobilisation Protocol will be carried out, which involves co-operation between Turkish Employment Agency (İŞKUR) and Turkish Union of Chambers and Commodity Exchanges (TOBB) to prepare the supply of labour for the jobs of the future in Turkey. The Protocol aims to facilitate stronger employment outcomes for job seekers through organised counselling, training, and job placement opportunities. Under this protocol, in addition to the provincial directorates and service centres of İŞKUR, the number of "İŞKUR Service Points" established within municipalities, social welfare institutions and other institutions and organisations will be increased by opening new İŞKUR Service Points.

Those who complete the courses and programmes with success will receive a certificate at the end of the course/programme and daily allowance and premiums of Insurance of Occupational Accidents and Professional Diseases and General Insurance will be paid by İŞKUR during the course/programme period. Within the scope of the protocol, it is also planned to deliver course for employees who do not have Professional Competence Certificate.

Stakeholder engagement and governance in the VET system

While the Ministry of National Education is the main overseer of the pre-tertiary vocational education, it regularly consults with stakeholders and other bodies that contribute to shaping up skills policies, through the following channels:

- *the National Advisory Council of Education*, which brings together a large number of policy makers and stakeholders every four years to discuss educational policy issues and to provide policy advice to the MoNE;
- *the Board of Training and Education*, which develops curricula, syllabi and learning objectives, and approves textbooks; and
- *the Vocational Education Council* (VEC), which decides on planning and development of VET programmes together with representatives from relevant ministries, trade and employers' unions and other key social partners (ETF, 2015). The VEC is the main high-level body of the government in VET area. It was established through the Law (No. 3308) on Vocational Education.

In addition, the Vocational Qualifications Authority (VQA) plays a critical role as the institution that is in charge of aligning VET qualifications with professional standards. However, the body has not delivered its full potential, as the process of defining qualifications for hundreds of occupations is still in progress.

Regional economic development actors

Turkey has a long tradition of development planning, going as far back as the introduction of five-year plans in the statist era of the 1930s. First, the outbreak of the Second World War and the political and economic developments in its aftermath interrupted planning exercises until the adoption of the new constitution in 1961. This constitution required governments to prepare development plans to inform and guide the private sector by making the development priorities and plans for public investments in infrastructure, mining, manufacturing, education, health and other spheres of social development publically known . The State Planning Organisation (SPO) was established for this purpose in 1961 and it was put in charge of preparing long-term and annual plans, following up on their implementation and advising on economic policy. The SPO reports directly to the Prime Minister's Office and the course of its actions and activities is set by the Supreme Planning Council, which is made up of relevant ministers and chaired by the Prime Minister.

Development plans include macroeconomic targets, social goals, and policy recommendations for individual subsectors of the economy. The targets set in plans are somewhat binding for the ministries and other public agencies but are only suggestive for private enterprises. Wide regional disparities between the eastern/south-eastern regions and the rest of the country have required the inclusion of regional issues in nationwide plans, making Turkey one of the first countries to develop regional planning.

The increasing complexity and diversification of the Turkish economy eventually necessitated the statutory reorganisation of the SPO into the Ministry of Development in 2011. The Ministry is an expert-based organisation which plans and guides Turkey's development process and focuses on the coordination of policies and strategy development.

For this purpose, the Ministry carries out a number of tasks, including steps to develop and implement policies and strategies for regional development, and to promote local actions by improving the policy-making capacity of regional and local actors.

When the SPO was converted into the Ministry of Development in 2011, legal grounds for the establishment of regional development agencies in all 26 NUTS2 regions had already been laid and a number of agencies had already begun their operations under the auspices of the organisation. Regional development agencies now operate in association with the Ministry of Development but each agency has its own legal entity and is liable to the provisions of civil law. There is also a common law that sets the mandates of all agencies. National co-ordination is handled by the Ministry of Development, which aims, among other things, to promote policies to reduce regional disparities.

The Ministry of Development monitors the activities of individual agencies, including planning, programming and allocation of grants to regional development projects. The main mission of regional agencies is to support, co-ordinate and guide the initiatives of regional actors to promote regional development; to identify sectoral development priorities; to serve as regional investment promotion agencies; and to mobilise regional resources and potentials while improving collaboration between actors in civil society and the public and private sectors.

Regional Development Boards guide the activities of regional development agencies and are made up of government officials serving in provinces covered in the mandate area, representatives of local municipalities, academics from regional universities, and private sector and NGO representatives. Day to day operations are handled by agency staff headed by a Secretary General appointed by the Ministry of Development. Development agencies are represented in PEVTBs and are expected to provide input to provincial skill development initiatives in accordance with provincial and regional development priorities.

Notes

1. For instance, in 2014, 46% of Turkish women between the ages of 15 and 29 were not engaged in employment or in any kind of training or educational pursuit. The corresponding percentage for males was just 17.2%.
2. Similar ideas are also echoed in the national strategy document for regional development covering 2014-2023 (Ministry of Development, 2014b).
3. The exact translation of "high school" in the Turkish language (and educational system) refers to a *vocational school* offering tertiary degrees under the administrative umbrella of a (public or private) university. The Turkish equivalent of what is called a "high school" in English is "lise" or lycée but in the rest of the document, the term "high school" will be used to refer to these upper-secondary schools or lycées, as in English.
4. The current law allows for the establishment and operation of privately funded universities only if they agree to be non-profit institutions of higher learning and bans them from seeking profits. All privately funded universities currently active in Turkey are non-profits and their tuition and other revenues are complemented by funding provided regularly by a foundation or endowment created by the founders.
5. The initiative is commonly referred to as the MLMM Project after (the acronym for) its motto which reads "Vocational Education: A Crucial Matter for the Nation" in Turkish.
6. In addition to training livestock farmers and others taking part in the supply chain in its training centre, Sütaş supports vocational education at the tertiary level through its co-operation agreements with Uludağ and Aksaray Universities.

References

Auer, P. and N. Popova (2003), "Labour market policy for restructuring in Turkey: The need for more active policies", *Employment paper* 2003/51, Intenational Labour Office, Geneva.

Carcillo, S. et al. (2015), "NEET Youth in the Aftermath of the Crisis: Challenges and Policies", *OECD Social, Employment and Migration Working Papers*, No. 164, OECD Publishing, Paris, http://dx.doi.org/10.1787/5js6363503f6-en.

Eurostat (2015), "Labour Force Survey" (database), http://ec.europa.eu/eurostat/data/database?node_code=lfsa_.

ILO Labour Statistics (2012), *Women and men in the informal economy*, http://laborsta.ilo.org/informal_economy_E.html, accessed on 24th February 2015.

İŞKUR (2015), *2015 Yılı Faaliyet Raporu* (Annual Activity Report), Ankara: İŞKUR, 2015.

Ministry of Development (2014a), *The 10th Development Plan 2014-2018*, Ankara: Ministry of Development of Turkey.

Ministry of Development (2014b), *Regional Development National Strategy 2014-2023*, Ankara: Ministry of Development of Turkey.

OECD (2017a), *Survey of Adult Skills* (PIAAC database), www.oecd.org/site/piaac/public dataandanalysis.htm.

OECD (2017b), "Education at a glance: Educational attainment and labour-force status", OECD Education Statistics (database), http://dx.doi.org/10.1787/889e8641-en.

OECD (2016a), *OECD Economic Surveys: Turkey 2016*, OECD Publishing, Paris, http://dx.doi.org/10.1787/eco_surveys-tur-2016-en.

OECD (2016b), *Aggregate National Accounts: Gross domestic product*, OECD National Accounts Statistics (database), http://dx.doi.org/10.1787/data-00001-en.

OECD (2016c), *Regional economy*, OECD Regional Statistics (database), http://dx.doi.org/10.1787/6b288ab8-en.

OECD (2016d), *Labour Market Statistics: Labour force statistics by sex and age: indicators*, OECD Employment and Labour Market Statistics (database), http://dx.doi.org/10.1787/data-00310-en.

OECD (2016e), *Regional labour markets*, OECD Regional Statistics (database), http://dx.doi.org/10.1787/f7445d96-en.

OECD (2016f), *Regional demography*, OECD Regional Statistics (database), http://dx.doi.org/10.1787/a8f15243-en.

OECD (2016g), *Turkey – Country Note – Skills Matter: Further Results from the Survey of Adult Skills*, OECD Skills Studies, OECD Publishing, Paris, www.oecd.org/skills/piaac/Skills-Matter-Turkey.pdf.

OECD (2015), *Education at a Glance*, OECD Education and Training Statistics (database), http://dx.doi.org/10.1787/edu-data-en.

OECD (2014), *Job Creation and Local Economic Development*, OECD Publishing, Paris, http://dx.doi.org/10.1787/9789264215009-en.

OECD (2012), *Large regions, TL2: Regional accounts*, OECD Regional Statistics (database), http://dx.doi.org/10.1787/data-00522-en.

Turkstat (2016a), *Labor Force Statistics* (statistical tables), www.turkstat.gov.tr/PreTablo.do?alt_id=1007.

Turkstat (2016b), *Address Based Population Registration System Results* (database), www.turkstat.gov.tr/PreTablo.do?alt_id=1059.

World Bank (2013), "Turkey: Evaluating the impact of IŞKUR's vocational training programs", Report No. 82306-TR, August 2013.

World Bank (2006), "Turkey Labor Market Study", Report No. 33254-TR, April 14, 2006.

Chapter 2

Overview of the Turkish case study areas

> To better understand the role of the local level in contributing to quality job creation, this study examines local activities in two provinces of Turkey: 1) Kocaeli; and 2) Trabzon. This chapter provides a labour market and economic overview of the provinces and their broader economic region. It also presents data and information on the supply and demand of skills at the sub-national level in Turkey

Overview

Turkey is divided into 12 regions, 26 (TL2) sub-regions and 81 (TL3) provinces (see Figure 2.1 below). In-depth fieldwork for this study was undertaken in the Turkish provinces of Kocaeli and Trabzon. These areas were selected after consultation between the OECD and İŞKUR. This chapter begins by giving a labour market and economic overview of the provinces. It concludes with the results of a tool developed by the OECD, which looks at the relationship between the supply and demand for skills at the sub-national level in Turkey.

Figure 2.1. **Provinces of Turkey**

East Marmara – North region and Kocaeli

The Kocaeli province is clustered together with Sakarya, Düzce, Bolu and Yalova under the Eastern Marmara-North sub-region (see Figure 2.1), characterised by a well-diversified economic structure and a strong manufacturing base. The broader East Marmara region (in which Kocaeli is located) in north-western Anatolia covers eight provinces and is a major hub of manufacturing activity and a leading region of origin for Turkish exports. The province of Kocaeli is home to a manufacturing industry that has grown rapidly over the past several decades (Kalkınma Bakanlığı, 2014).

The industrial base of the province allows for the production of a wide range of goods, including relatively high value-added products in the oil refinery and automobile industries. Enviably located between the major industrial centres of İstanbul, Sakarya, Adapazarı and Bursa, Kocaeli is the leading province in its sub-region in terms of the volume of economic activity and income levels. It is bordered by Marmara Sea on the East and the Black Sea on the North. With a population of about 1.7 million, it represented about 2.2% of the population of Turkey in 2014. Its central district is İzmit, a major industrial town itself and a leading export hub with modern port facilities located by the Gulf of İzmit. With annual exports exceeding USD 9 billion, Kocaeli comes second only to Istanbul, the country's commercial and cultural centre.

Kocaeli also benefits from its proximity to the three largest metropolises in the country. This gives the province a crucial advantage in terms of access to major domestic markets. With more than 14 million inhabitants in 2015, İstanbul's city centre is just an hour bus ride from İzmit, while Ankara and İzmir, whose population exceeded 5 million and 4 million respectively in 2015, are both less than 500 kilometres (300 miles) away.

Figure 2.2. **Sectoral composition of employment (%), Eastern Marmara – North region, 2007-15**

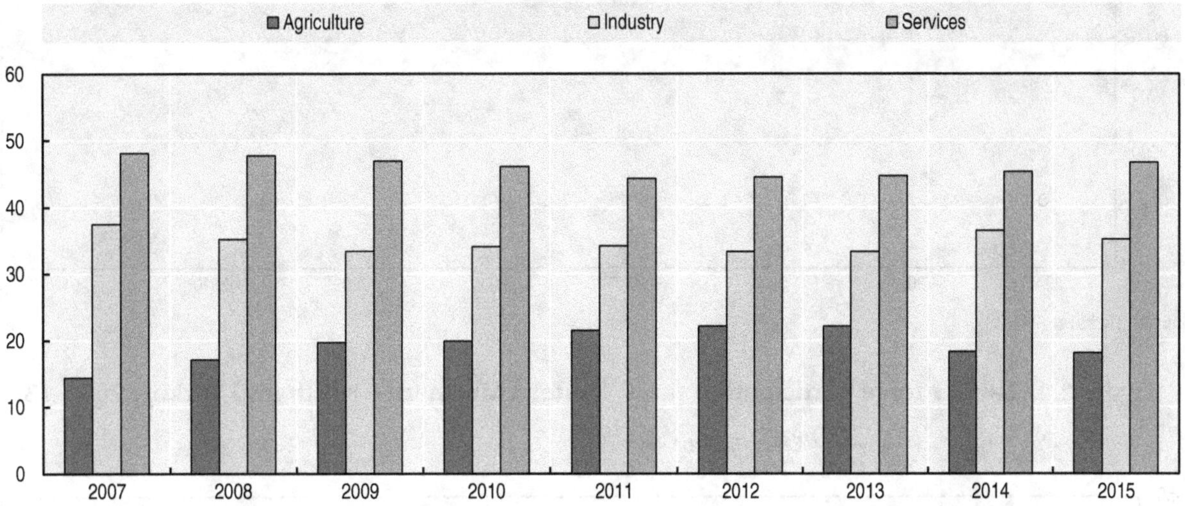

Source: Turkstat (2016a).

The province has two well-established free trade zones (FTZ) and attracts substantial amounts of foreign direct investment, particularly through large scale automotive projects. Kocaeli is also home to the largest oil refinery in Turkey and 13 industrial zones scattered across the province offer the infrastructure needed for the production of a wide range of manufacturing products. Due to the intensity of manufacturing activity (especially in the Izmit and Gebze districts), per capita electricity consumption in Kocaeli is almost three times as high as the national average. Agricultural activity is relatively low with 85 000 hectares of land used in agriculture, which amounts to less than 18% of the region's total (Turkstat, 2014a). As a result of the region's industrial importance, Gross Value Added per capita is significantly higher than the country average (see Figure 2.3 below).

In terms of employment trends in the region, the labour force participation rate in Eastern Marmara – North was close to 55% in 2013, while the employment rate stood at around 49%. Between 2009 and 2013, the labour force participation rate rose by approximately eight percentage points and the employment rate increased by roughly nine percentage points, which are both positive signs for increasing the overall supply of people who are available to work in the labour market (See Figures 2.4 and 2.5).

At approximately 10%, the unemployment rate in Eastern Marmara – North sits around the national average in Turkey. Looking at historical trends, the unemployment rate in Eastern Marmara – North fell from 17% to nearly 10% from 2006-13. This recovery came after a sudden rise in unemployment between the years 2008 and 2009 caused by the Global Financial Crisis (Turkstat, 2014a). Due mostly to the sudden and substantial shrinkage of the European automotive market during the recession, Kocaeli was hit more severely than the rest of Turkey by the Global Financial Crisis (see Figure 2.6).

Figure 2.3. **Annual value-added per person (USD at current prices), Eastern Marmara-North region and Turkey, 2004-11**

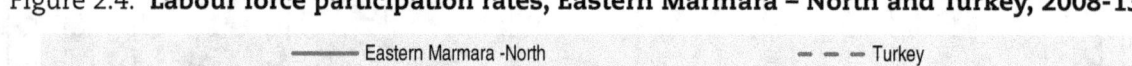

Source: Turkstat (2016b).

Figure 2.4. **Labour force participation rates, Eastern Marmara – North and Turkey, 2008-13**

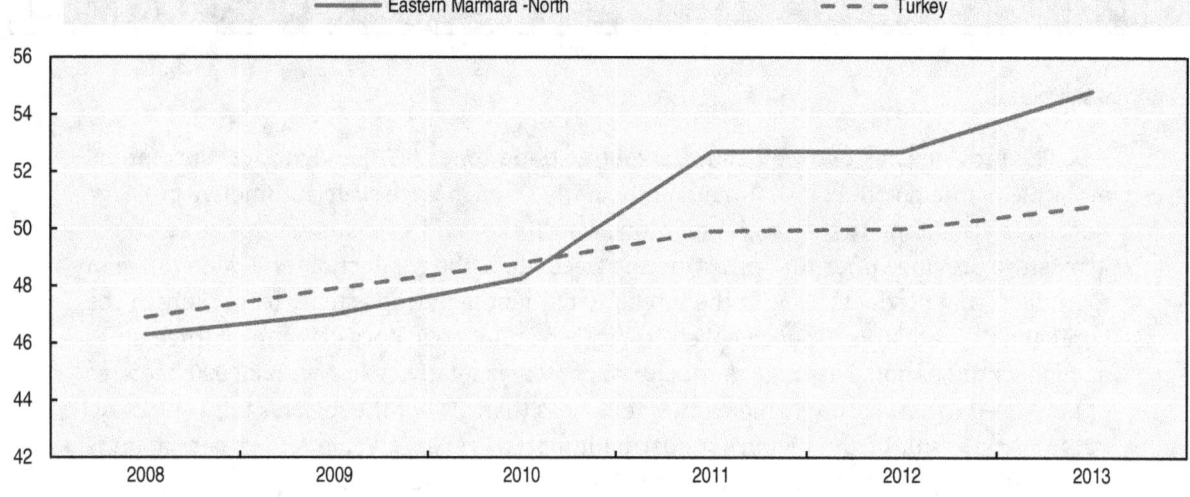

Source: Turkstat (2016a).

The Eastern Marmara – North region shows relatively fast demographic growth due not only to local fertility but also to immigration from other regions of the country. The incoming and outgoing migration rates were 2.97% and 2.05% respectively in 2014, implying a net inflow of people from other provinces. Migrants are mostly young people in search of employment opportunities and better living conditions. For instance, the largest share (16.5%) of migrants Kocaeli received between 2011 and 2012 were 20-24 year olds, followed by 25-29 year olds (15.3%). This contributes to the dynamism of the province's labour market. Nonetheless, a closer look at outgoing migration hints at a net human resource loss due to internal migration, with a significant minority (18.9%) of the population seeking to settle outside the region between 2011 and 2012 being tertiary educated (MARKA, 2013). This indicates that retaining skilled labour is a challenge for Kocaeli.

Figure 2.5. **Employment rates, Eastern Marmara – North and Turkey, 2008-13**

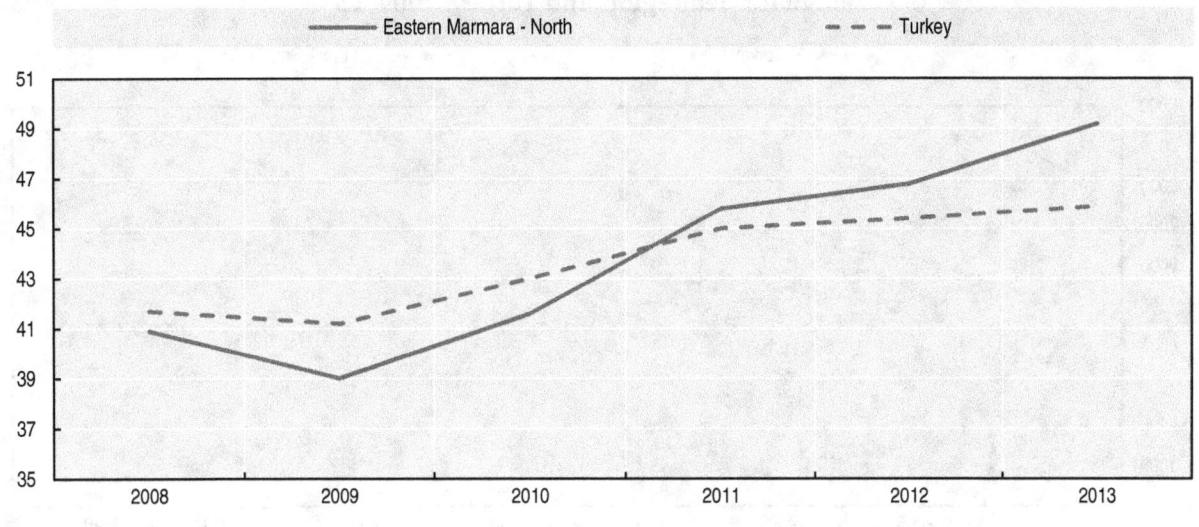

Source: Turkstat (2016a).

Figure 2.6. **Unemployment rates, Kocaeli province and Turkey, 2008-13**

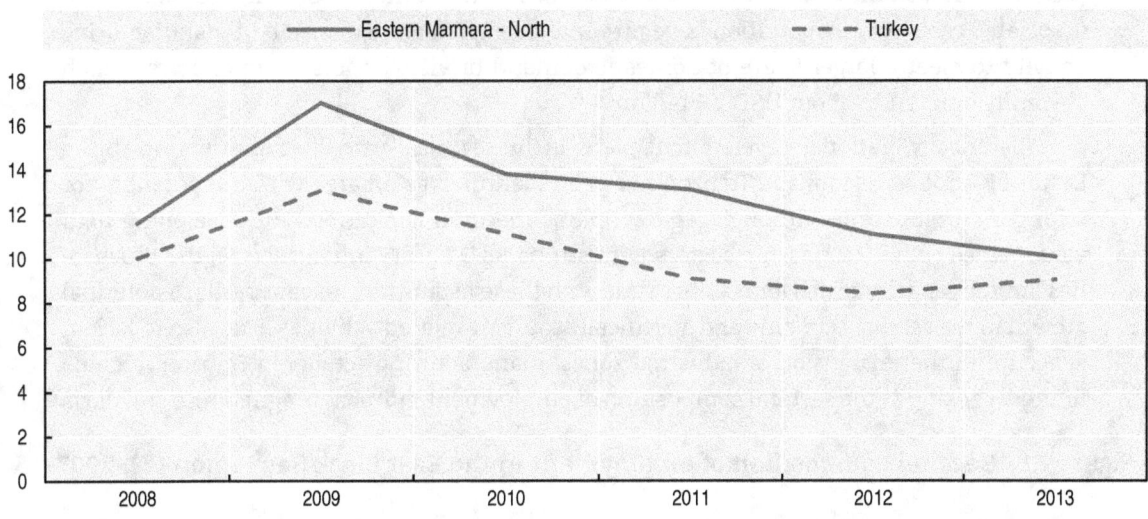

Source: Turkstat (2016a).

East Black Sea region and Trabzon

The East Black Sea region is made up of eight provinces. Located in north-eastern Turkey, along the coastal line of the Black Sea, Trabzon is a province with a population of about 800 000, close to 1% of the country's total population. Production activity in the Eastern Black Sea region is dominated by farming and animal husbandry. Sectoral diversification is limited, and the relatively small volume of manufacturing activity is concentrated on mostly low value-added products (DOKA, 2014a).[1] Unlike the East Marmara – North region, annual value-added per person is significantly lower than the national average (see Figure 2.7).

There has been suggestions that Trabzon should be given a central role to drive larger regional development, based in part on the potential benefits that might be reaped from the revival of the province's large seaport capacity and new business opportunities that were thought to arise following the establishment of the province's free trade zone in 1992

Figure 2.7. **Annual value-added per person (USD at current prices), East Black Sea region and Turkey, 2004-11**

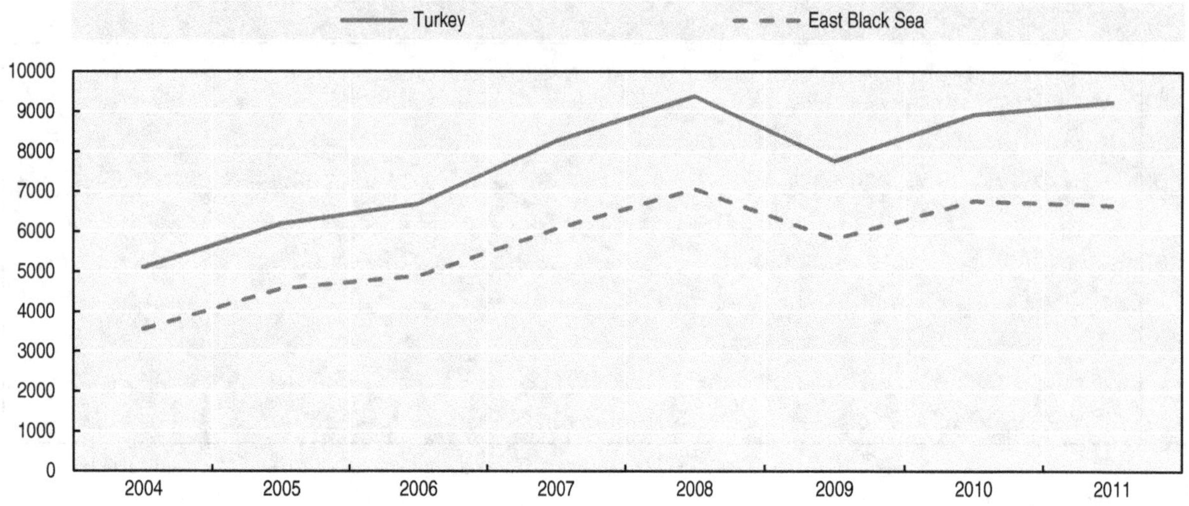

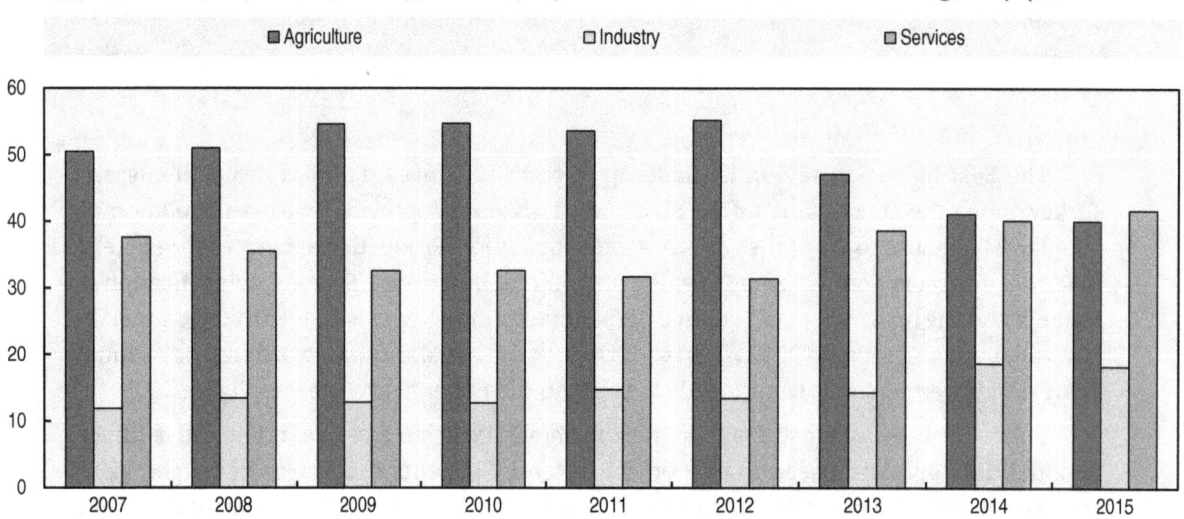

Source: Turkstat (2016b).

(with a trade volume of about USD 120 million). Yet, the difficulty of land access and the associated costs of transportation have prevented a significant expansion of manufacturing activity to meet a larger share of domestic demand or visible increase in exports, which currently amount to about USD 1.3 billion.

Historically, national development plans in Turkey have paid special attention to the Eastern Black Sea region, and Trabzon has been identified as an area with the potential for stronger development. Although regional plans mention aspirations for developing high value-added activities, flagship sectors with strong R&D and IT infrastructure, the province has limited capacity to deliver results in line with these aspirations, except perhaps potential growth in the service economy and specifically tourism-related activities. Due also to lack of space for further expansion of industrial zones, manufacturing activity in Trabzon remains limited. Looking at the sectoral composition of employment in Trabzon, agriculture still plays

Figure 2.8. **Sectoral composition of employment in the East Black Sea region (%), 2007-15**

Source: Turkstat (2016a).

Figure 2.9. **Panel of labour force participation, employment and unemployment rates (respectively), East Black Sea region and Turkey, 2008-13**

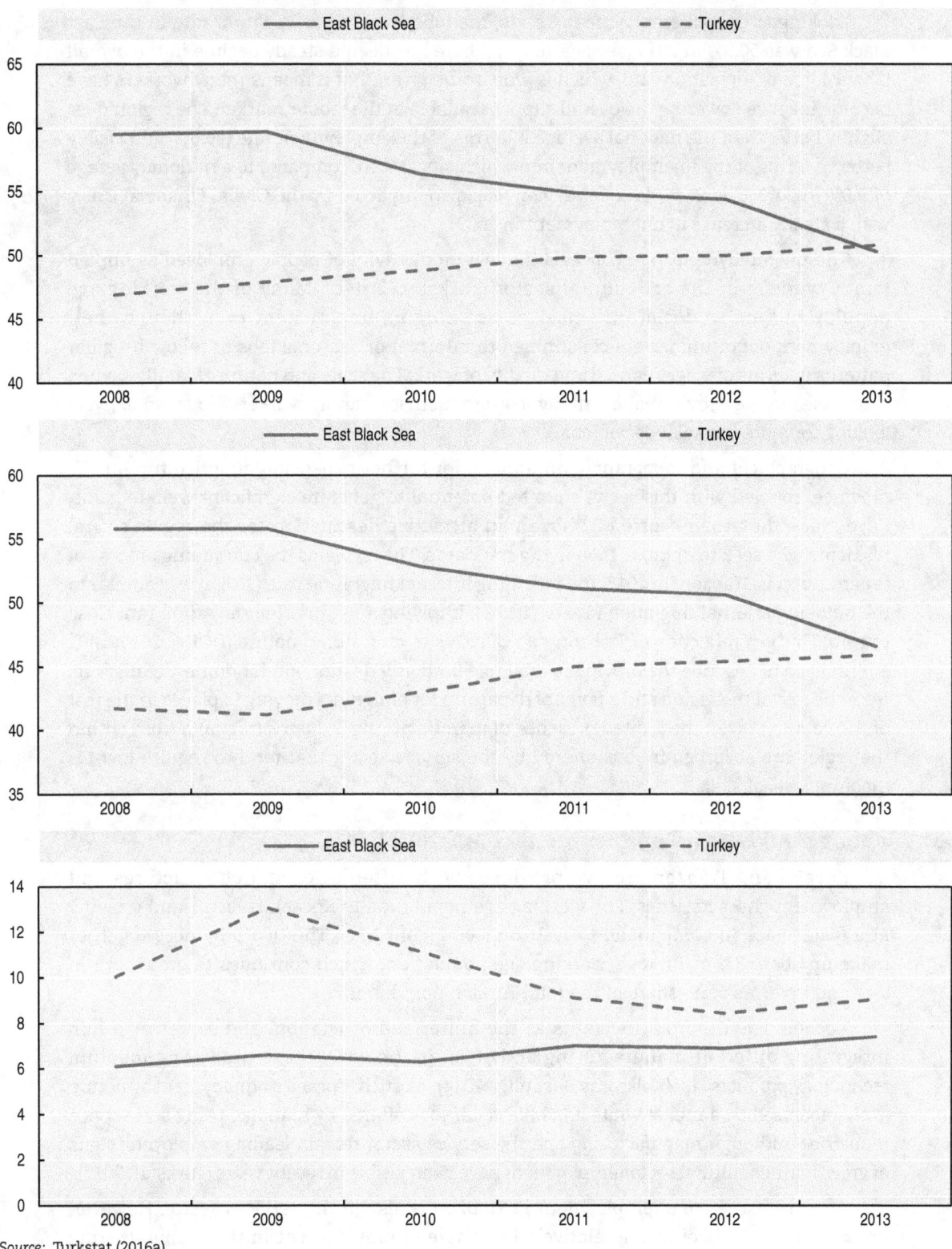

Source: Turkstat (2016a).

a large role as a key sector, compared to the industry and services sector. From 2007-13, the services sector has increased in its overall share of employment (see Figure 2.8).

Looking at overall employment trends, the labour force participation rate in the East Black Sea was 50.3% in 2013 (see Figure 2.9). There has been a steady decline in the overall labour force participation rate, which is worrisome given that it means many workers have become inactive, lowering the overall supply available in the labour market. The region does slightly better than the national average in terms of the employment rate (46.6%) and visibly better in terms of the unemployment rate which sits at 7.4% compared to a national average of 9.6% in 2013. The East Black Sea region was also impacted by the Global Financial Crisis with a steady increase in unemployment in 2009.

The unemployment rate conceals the low productivity of people employed as unpaid family workers in the agricultural sector (Turkstat, 2014b). Many of the working age population tend to declare themselves as being in employment even though their employment opportunities are constrained to informal or seasonal jobs or follow irregular patterns in terms of wages earned and quality of work. The scale and nature of family-owned businesses in the province allow many low-productivity "family workers" to avoid actively looking for more formal types of jobs.

Geographical and topographic limitations for further expansion of agriculture in the province, coupled with this sector's limited potential to generate significant welfare gains, have made the urban centre of Trabzon an attractive destination for the region's rural residents who seek to improve their living standards. This explains the continuing process of urbanisation in Trabzon. In 2013, the incoming internal migration rate (1.18%) was similar to the outgoing internal migration rate of (1.11%), implying a net internal migration rate close to zero. This is a reflection of Trabzon's so called "stepping stone" nature (DOKA, 2014a: 40), a term used to describe the province's dual role both as a destination for domestic migrants from the rest of the region and a point of departure for emigrants moving to places in the rest of the country. Given the limited presence of manufacturing industry, migrants from within the region are absorbed in jobs offered by the service sector that tend to require low-to-medium level of skills.

Local labour markets and employment characteristics

Kocaeli and Trabzon are two provinces with different economic structures and employment characteristics. The working age population in Kocaeli is larger and growing at a faster pace in comparison to Trabzon (see Figure 2.12). The two provinces together make up about 3% of Turkey's working age population, which continues to grow both in size and in terms of its share of the total Turkish population.

Kocaeli benefits from its status as the hinterland of İstanbul and serves as a hub integrating different manufacturing activities, particularly those producing medium technology products (T.C. Kalkınma Bakanlığı, 2014). As such, Kocaeli's employment structure is characterised by a mix of white and blue collar jobs offered by manufacturing and service industries. Although manufacturing and the service sector remain leading employers, signs of growth in agricultural sector employment have been visible in recent years (Turkstat, 2013).

The highest share of employment in Trabzon is also in the services sector. However, unlike Kocaeli, Trabzon has a relatively low share of employment in the manufacturing industry. The province is the export hub of the region, with farming and animal husbandry accounting for far the largest share of the province's exports (69%) (DOKA, 2014a). While

Figure 2.10. **Working age population (15-64 year old) in Kocaeli and Trabzon, 2007-16**

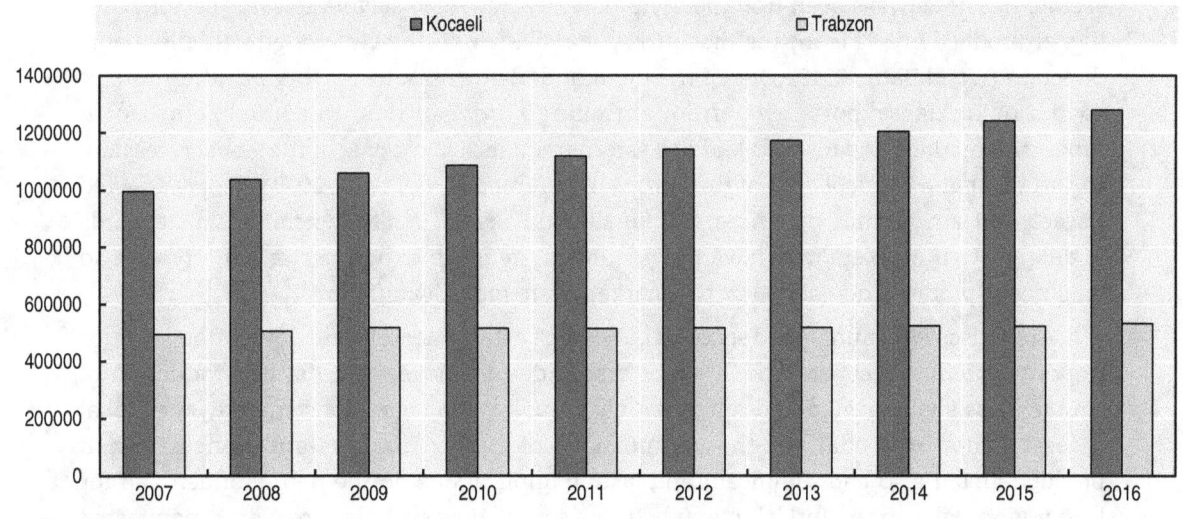

Source: Turkstat (2016c).

Trabzon is the main port for exports of agriculture-based products, Rize and Ordu are the main regional centres of agricultural production. This sector's impact on employment cannot be fully accounted for due to the seasonal and undeclared nature of employment in agricultural activities in Turkey.

Manufacturing employment is provided mostly by small and medium-sized enterprises (SMEs) that typically produce low-tech to medium-low tech products such as processed food and textiles. As such, local labour markets are mostly driven by low- to medium-skilled job dynamics. Still, compared to the other provinces in its region, Trabzon provides more and a wider range of opportunities for employment. The intensifying need to meet the demands of a growing population and the geographical limitations to agriculture have prompted internal migration from rural parts of Trabzon to the main urban centre of the province, posing particular challenges linked to urbanisation of the city.

Development plans have so far focused on turning the province into a regional hub in a limited number of activities. Therefore, Trabzon's growth strategy as envisaged by DOKAP, the main regional development plan, and in similar plans drafted by the regional development agency, is actively tilting towards construction and tourism and hospitality activities (İŞKUR, 2014b)[2]. Thanks to investments, the share of employment in services is on the rise. Employment growth in the service industries can partly be explained by the emergence of the potential of relatively untapped tourism and real estate development sectors, due particularly to demand coming from the neighbouring countries and the Gulf countries of the Arab world.

Impact of the economic climate and employment policies

As explained in the previous chapter, Turkey enjoyed rapid growth rates in the aftermath of the 2001 crisis until the global economic crisis. Following a strong recovery in 2010 and 2011, the Turkish economy grew at an average rate of 6.1% annually between 2012 and 2014. Employment grew at an average rate of 3.8% annually between 2009 and 2015, and more than five million new jobs were created during this period (OECD, 2015).

Despite such positive developments, the movement of labour between non-agricultural sectors has not always been from poorly productive, low-tech sectors towards sectors with higher productivity. This means that Turkey is moving only slowly in a growth-enhancing direction (World Bank, 2013). One of the main underlying reasons for this was the strategic switch of Turkish exports away from shrinking European (and to some extent North American) markets and towards Middle Eastern markets at the onset of the global recession. In particular, the near collapse of the European automobile market in 2009 strongly affected Kocaeli and surrounding provinces, like Bursa and Sakarya. While switching focus towards Middle Eastern markets may have provided some relief to export sectors, the types and qualities of products demanded by the markets were radically different.

After discovering untapped sections of Middle Eastern markets with lower standards for imported products, some Turkish exporters tended to move towards the production of simpler, less sophisticated and relatively lower-quality products. Consequently, the global recession not only changed the composition of export markets and hence Turkish production, but also had significant and lasting implications on the nature of demand for labour (and skills) in the Turkish manufacturing sector. How such developments manifested themselves in local economies can be analysed in terms of overall employment policies, the role of regional actors in providing employment services and the education levels of Kocaeli and Trabzon.

In Kocaeli, in line with the nature of economic activities in the region, the employment share of manufacturing remained largely constant between 2008 and 2012 (34.1% on average). While the service sector experienced a decline in its employment share from 47.7% to 44.5% over the same period, it remained the leading employer. In terms of productivity, the regional gross value-added per person (output based calculation) was about USD 13 100 as of 2011 – significantly higher than the national average of USD 9 200 for the same year. In terms of total value-added, the region has contributed about 6% of the total regional value-added in Turkey between 2007 and 2011. The largest contributor to regional output was the service sector, which produced 57.1% of the regional value-added per person in 2011 (Turkstat, 2014a). As expected, productivity of the service sector is higher than average, as reflected by its much lower employment share – which stood at 44.3% the same year.

The sectoral distribution of economic activities and employment in the region was also discussed in the regional development plan (2014-23) prepared by the East Marmara Regional Development Agency (MARKA). The plan emphasises the need for specialisation and suggests selecting the priority sectors to develop in the region based on four criteria: investment intensity, employment volume, export volume, and value-added generated. Specific employment policies with regards to the leading sectors are spelled out in the plan within the context of human capital development. When looked at from such a perspective, basic employment indicators, while remaining above national averages, lag behind the EU27 averages (MARKA, 2014). The plan, therefore, envisions raising education and skills levels of the population in order to increase both the productivity of the workforce and employment levels. Within this context, it highlights collaboration between different vocational education and training (VET) actors as a critical success factor to improving skills.

Despite this emphasis on VET as a channel for strengthening labour markets, no sector-specific policies have been suggested in the regional plan. Filling the types of vacant jobs typically offered in the province requires people who have acquired adequate vocational skills through education and work experience (MARKA, 2014). In Kocaeli, vacant jobs for which workforce recruitment is particularly difficult are concentrated mostly in the manufacturing sector (İŞKUR, 2014a). Hence, aligning vocational education and training with the needs of the local labour market and taking steps towards increasing the popularity of this type of education are identified by the plan as key skills development areas. However, specific or concrete actions are not outlined beyond pointing to the need to track regional labour market trends and developing relevant strategies to improve VET.

For Trabzon, the employment outlook is difficult to map out since no data on sectoral and occupational distribution of employment at the provincial level are available. It is imperative to analyse the region first to identify key economic trends. The 2007-13 averages of the employment shares in manufacturing and services were 13.3% and 34.4%, respectively. At 47.1% in 2013, agriculture had a higher average share of employment both the manufacturing and services sectors. Manufacturing activity in the region is mostly focused on food processing (DOKA, 2014a). This economic structure produced a per capita gross value-added figure of about USD 6 600 in 2011, well below the national average of USD 9 200, placing the region in the 17th out of the 26 regions in Turkey (Turkstat, 2014b). The regional output share was slightly higher than the national average in agriculture (12.7% compared to 9.0%), slightly lower in the manufacturing industry (23.1% versus 27.5%) and slightly higher in services (64.2% versus 63.5%), according to Turkstat figures. Trabzon itself is also a largely service economy due mainly to topographic and geographic conditions that provide limited room for agricultural development and manufacturing. As a result, the town has a mostly service-oriented labour market, though the service industry is probably not as sophisticated as it is in Kocaeli.

The regional plan of the East Black Sea Development Agency (DOKA) identifies various problems preventing increases in employment, varying from limitations of human capital to geography. However, the plan does not elaborate any specific strategies. One notable exception is the detailed analysis of tourism activities in the region where Trabzon is located (DOKA, 2014a). Another sector-specific report prepared by the agency (DOKA, 2014b) assesses the potential developmental contribution of tourist inflow from the Arab world, particularly the Gulf area, and urges local authorities to develop policies by placing Trabzon at the heart of such efforts. While neither their employment-boosting effects nor skills shortages are satisfactorily discussed in the report, tourism related activities are regarded as key to the income generation potential of Trabzon's economy and subsequent development.

Regional actors have limited opportunities to contribute to the process of drafting and implementing region- or province-specific employment policies and concrete action plans. The highly centralised structure of the Turkish administrative system, lack of inter-agency co-ordination, and significant discrepancies in the delivery capacity of central and local agents often hinder the local formulation and implementation of major employment initiatives. As is the case with regional development agencies, the responsibility for devising sectoral policies for local development and employment generation at the local level is often the responsibility of central government. Such policies are expected to be designed at the national level and implemented through provincial representatives of ministries and other state agencies.

Education and training

Education levels in Kocaeli and Trabzon vary considerably. Although the net schooling rates for primary and secondary level education do not differ greatly, there are visible differences between vocational and tertiary education rates. The importance of upper secondary and tertiary education for the labour market is multi-fold, with effects on labour force participation, unemployment rates and wages. OECD data shows, for instance, that on average, over 80% of tertiary-educated people in the OECD countries are employed, in contrast to around 70% of people with an upper secondary or post-secondary non-tertiary education.

The data also reveals that unemployment rates tend to be lower among individuals with vocational upper secondary or post-secondary non-tertiary education (8%) than among adults with a general upper secondary education (9%). As for the difference in wages earned, the Turkish case is a stark example, as the country has one of the highest earnings premiums for upper secondary and tertiary education. In 2013, adults with tertiary degrees earned 88% more on average than adults with upper secondary education, while this premium was on average 60% in the OECD as a whole (OECD, 2015). Yet, the size of the group collecting wage premiums on tertiary education relative to the total adult population is not as large in Turkey as it is in the OECD.

As for the relative educational standing of the provinces of Kocaeli and Trabzon within Turkey, basic education indicators do not show significant discrepancies. Both provinces perform well and surpass national averages in schooling and literacy rates (6 years and over). The net schooling rate for primary education (2013-2014) was 99.7% in both Kocaeli and Trabzon, which is slightly higher than the national average (99.6%). In 2013, Kocaeli (97.2%) performed better than Trabzon (94.9%) in terms of the literacy rate (Turkstat, 2014b).

A different outlook emerges when looking at the number of student enrolled in tertiary or higher degree programmes (see Figure 2.11), where Kocaeli has a much larger number of students enrolled compared to Trabzon. Looking more specifically at VET resources, Kocaeli had more schools (166), teachers (3 603), and students (65 302) in 2013-14 than Trabzon: 94, 2 108, and 29 334 respectively (Turkstat, 2014a and 2014b). These numbers alone do not signal the importance attributed to VET, given the differences in terms of demography and the structure of local economies in these two provinces.

Figure 2.11. **Number of students enrolled in tertiary and higher degree programmes: Kocaeli and Trabzon**

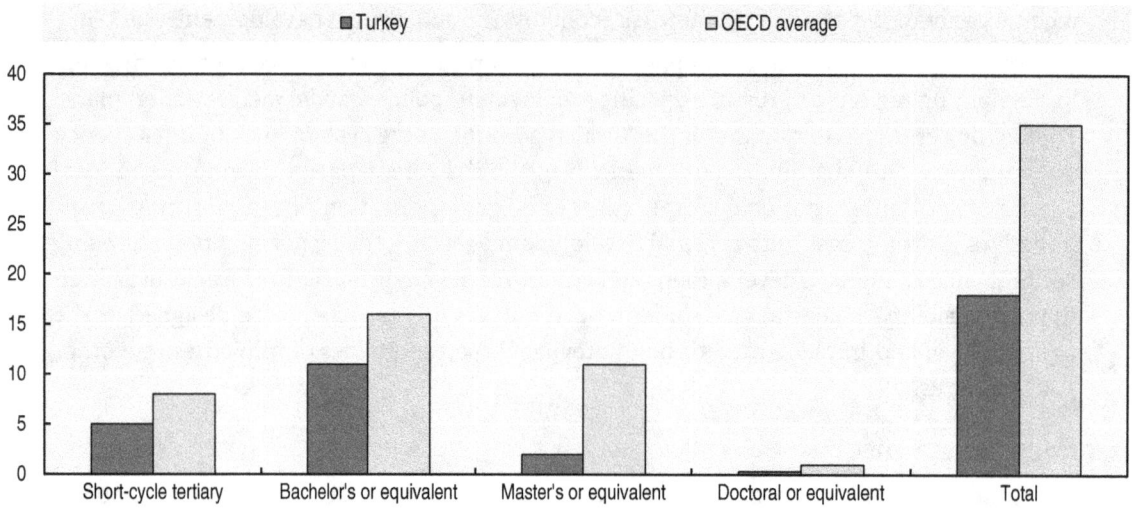

Source: Higher Education Council (YÖK) Statistics.

Kocaeli hosts 2% of all graduates of tertiary education institutions in Turkey, while Trabzon hosts 1.5%. Both provinces have universities with a large numbers of students. While the major state university, Kocaeli University (KU) has over 75 000 students, only a fraction (approximately 9 000) are residents in the province. The university's vocational schools have 21 different departments in which more than 4 000 students are enrolled. The province also hosts Gebze Higher Technology Institute (GYTE), which specialises in research and technology production and featured over 2 000 students in bachelor's degree programmes as of 2013-14 (Kocaeli Ticaret Odası, 2014). Adding to Kocaeli's technical and vocational capabilities at the tertiary education level, there are two technology parks, creating an eco-system along with the organised industry zones.

Trabzon's state university is a technical university, where more students are enrolled in engineering and science programmes than in humanities and social sciences. Due to insufficient investment in technological infrastructure and to the weakness of the local industry, the education provided falls short of making a marked contribution to the skills levels in the local labour market, as noted in the regional development plan (DOKAP).

There is significant variation in participation and graduation rates for the vocational training courses provided within the scope of İŞKUR's active labour market programmes. İŞKUR's courses are classified as training courses with employment guarantees and general workforce development courses. Over the period between 2009 and 2013, a total of 62 employment guaranteed courses were opened in Kocaeli with 1 503 participants. During the same time period, nearly 13 000 participants were trained in 573 general employment courses. In addition, a total of 3 864 apprentices/apprenticeship trainees and 403 senior apprentices completed their education between 2013 and 2014 through Vocational Training Centres under the direction of the province's governorship and district administrations (İŞKUR, 2014a). In Trabzon, 835 participants were enrolled in 48 employment guaranteed courses during the period 2009-13, and there were an additional 254 general employment courses with 4 334 participants (İŞKUR, 2014b).

The gap between Kocaeli and Trabzon is even more evident in terms of UMEM courses (for the five-year period following the project's inception). In Kocaeli, 7 166 students began to receive theoretical training (out of a quota of 8,421 set for student take-in for these courses),

Figure 2.12. **Attendance to capacity ratios for UMEM courses in Kocaeli and Trabzon, 2011-16**

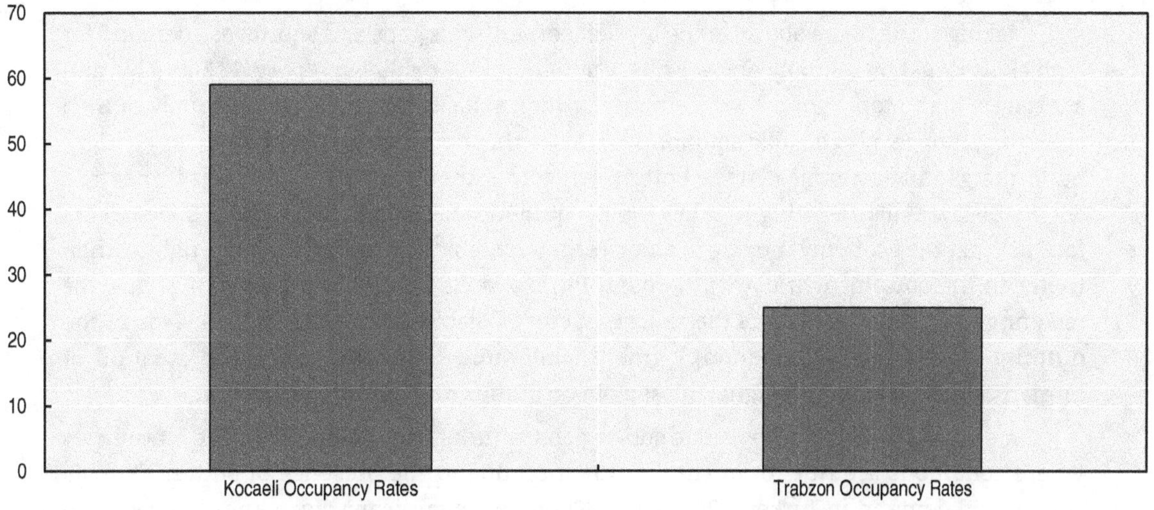

Source: UMEM Database.

and 5 459 successfully graduated. In Trabzon, on the other hand, 1 002 students began to receive theoretical training (out of the student take-in quota of 1 142) with 676 successfully graduating (UMEM, 2015). The two provinces were also different in terms of the interest shown for these courses. In 2013, there were 47 UMEM courses opened with only 290 participants (Turkstat, 2014b) in Trabzon, whereas the numbers for the same year in Kocaeli were 216 UMEM courses with 3605 participants (Turkstat, 2014a).

Mapping skills supply and demand in Turkey

To supplement the analysis above, the OECD has developed a statistical tool to understand the balance between skills supply and demand within local labour markets (Froy, Giguère and Meghnagi, 2012). In the Turkish context, this tool can supplement the previous analysis to provide policy makers with an understanding of potential skills mismatches that may be occurring at the sub-national level. It can also inform place-based policy approaches at the local level.

Figure 2.13. **Understanding the relationship between skills supply and demand**

	Skills supply (low)	Skills supply (high)
Skills demand (high)	SKILLS GAPS AND SHORTAGES	HIGH SKILL EQUILIBRIUM
Skills demand (low)	LOW SKILL EQUILIBRIUM	SKILLS SURPLUS

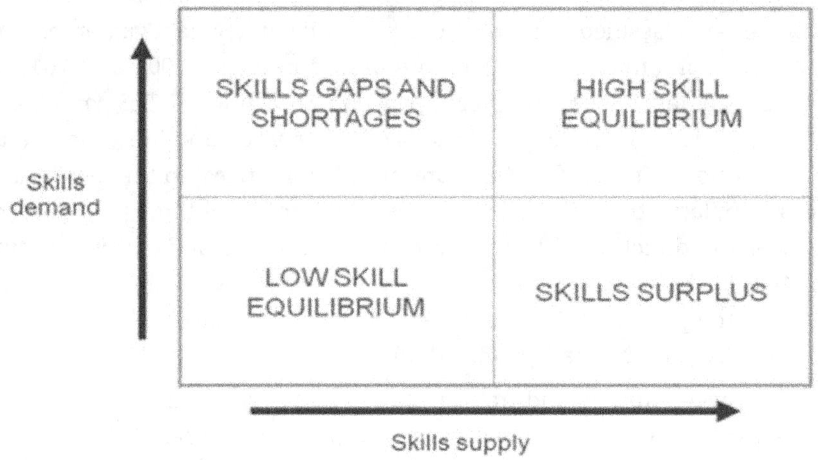

Source: Froy, F. and S. Giguère (2010).

Looking at the figure above, in the top-left corner (skills gaps and shortages), demand for high skills is met by a supply of low skills, a situation that results in reported skills gaps and shortages. In the top-right corner, demand for high skills is met by an equal supply of high skills, resulting in a high-skills equilibrium. This is the most desired destination for all high-performing local economies. At the bottom-left corner the demand for low skills is met by a supply of low skills resulting in a low-skills equilibrium. The challenge that policymakers face is to get the economy moving in a north-easterly direction towards the top-right corner. Lastly, in the bottom-right corner, demand for low skills is met by a supply of high skills resulting in an economy where the skills capacity available is not utilised. This leads to the outmigration of talent, underemployment, skills under-utilisation and the attrition of human capital, all of which signal missed opportunities for creating prosperity.

This typology has been applied to sub-regions in Turkey (see Figure 2.14). The map shows where conditions are ripe for quality job creation due to the presence of both high skills supply and demand in Turkey's 26 regions. There is a significant divergence between the

2. OVERVIEW OF THE TURKISH CASE STUDY AREAS

> **Box 2.1. Explaining the diagnostic tool**
>
> The analysis is carried out at Territorial Level 3 regions (regions with populations ranging between 150 000 and 800 000). The supply of skills was measured by the percentage of the population with post-secondary education. The demand for skills was measured by the percentage of the population employed in medium-high skilled occupations and its productivity level (GVA per worker). Regions are also classified in relation to the average state unemployment rate. The indices are standardised using the inter-decile method and are compared with the national median. Further explanations on the methodology can be found in Froy, Giguère and Meghnagi, 2012.
>
> Source: Froy, F., S. Giguère and M. Meghnagi (2012), "Skills for Competitiveness: A Synthesis Report", OECD Local Economic and Employment Development (LEED) Working Papers, No. 2012/09, OECD Publishing, http://dx.doi.org/10.1787/5k98xwskmvr6-en.

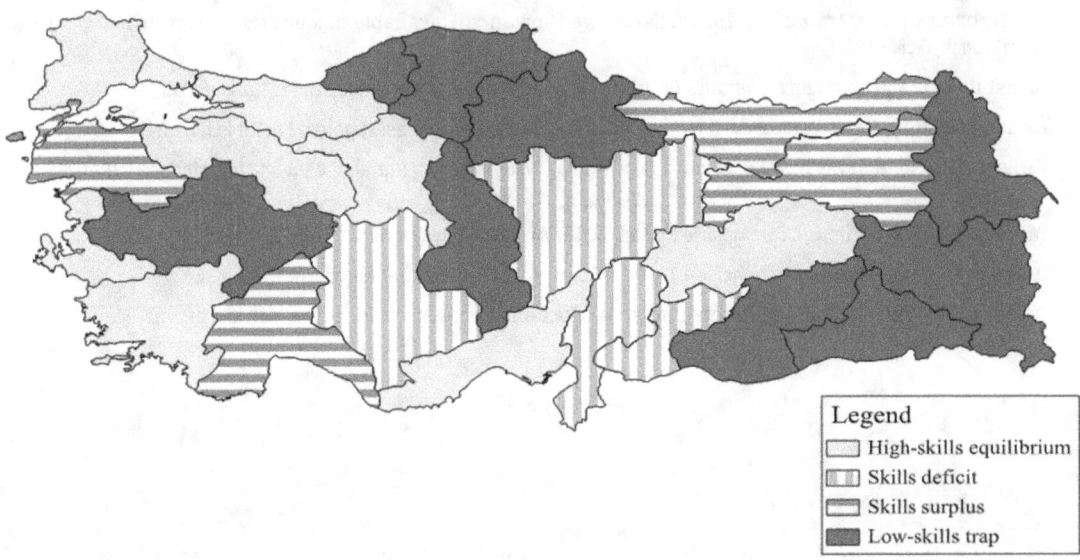

Figure 2.14. **Balancing skills supply and demand in Turkey, 2014**

Legend:
- High-skills equilibrium
- Skills deficit
- Skills surplus
- Low-skills trap

Source: OECD (2016).

Western and the Central-Eastern parts of the country. The area between Istanbul and Ankara and the area near the Mediterranean and the Aegean are mostly in a "high-skills equilibrium", where a high supply of skills (percentage of people with post-secondary education) is matched by a high skills demand (the percentage of medium and high skills occupations and GVA per worker). Adana, Malatya and Erzurum are in a skills surplus (where skills supply exceeds demand) and Zonguldak in a skills deficit (where skills demand exceeds supply). The remaining regions are in "low-skills equilibrium" (where a low supply of skills is matched by low demand).

Notes

1. Main industry branches in the region are food, wood products, non-metal furniture products and medical devices. Product diversification in the region followed a declining trend between 2003 and 2009 as noted in Kalkınma Bakanlığı (2014).

2. By İŞKUR's Trabzon Labour Market Demand Survey, out of 2 143 firms contacted, 574 operate in the construction sector.

References

Froy, F. and S. Giguère (2010), "Putting in Place Jobs that Last: A Guide to Rebuilding Quality Employment at Local Level", *OECD Local Economic and Employment Development (LEED) Working Papers*, No. 2010/13, OECD Publishing, http://dx.doi.org/10.1787/5km7jf7qtk9p-en.

Froy, F., S. Giguère and M. Meghnagi (2012), "Skills for Competitiveness: A Synthesis Report", *OECD Local Economic and Employment Development (LEED) Working Papers*, No. 2012/09, OECD Publishing, http://dx.doi.org/10.1787/5k98xwskmvr6-en.

Higher Education Council (YÖK) Statistics (2016), https://istatistik.yok.gov.tr/.

ISKUR (2014a), *Kocaeli 2014 İşgücü Piyasası Araştırma Raporu*, Kocaeli Çalışma ve İş Kurumu İl Müdürlüğü.

İŞKUR (2014b), *Trabzon 2014 İşgücü Piyasası Araştırma Raporu*, Trabzon Çalışma ve İş Kurumu İl Müdürlüğü.

MARKA (2013), *Doğu Marmara Bölgesi Demografik Yapısı ve İç Göç Hareketleri*, Kocaeli: MARKA.

OECD (2016), "Turkey", in Job Creation and Local Economic Development 2016, OECD Publishing, Paris, http://dx.doi.org/10.1787/9789264261976-45-en.

OECD (2015), *OECD Employment and Labour Market Statistics* (database), http://dx.doi.org/ 10.1787/lfs-data-en.

T.C. Kalkınma Bakanlığı (2014), *Bölgesel Ulusal Gelişim Stratejisi 2014-2023*, Ankara: T.C. Kalkınma Bakanlığı.

T.C. Trabzon Valiliği, Trabzon'da Tarım, Sanayi ve Hayvancılık available at *www.trabzon.gov.tr/index.php?p=icerik_&cid=122*.

Turkstat (2016a), *Labor Force Statistics* (statistical tables), www.turkstat.gov.tr/PreTablo.do?alt_id=1007.

Turkstat (2016b), *Gross Value Added by regions* (database), www.turkstat.gov.tr/PreTablo.do?alt_id=1075.

Turkstat (2016c), *Address Based Population Registration System Results* (database), www.turkstat.gov.tr/PreTablo.do?alt_id=1059.

Turkstat (2014a), *Seçilmiş Göstergelerle Kocaeli 2013*, Ankara: Türkiye İstatistik Kurumu.

Turkstat (2014b), *Seçilmiş Göstergelerle Trabzon 2013*, Ankara: Türkiye İstatistik Kurumu.

Turkstat (2013), *Regional Directorate Statistics, Kocaeli*, Kocaeli: Türkiye İstatistik Kurumu Kocaeli İl Müdürlüğü.

Chapter 3

Local Job Creation Dashboard findings in Turkey

> *This chapter highlights findings from the local job creation dashboard, which is a policy assessment tool developed by the OECD that was applied in Trabzon and Kocaeli. The findings are discussed through the four thematic areas of the study: 1) better aligning policies and programmes to local employment development; 2) adding value through skills; 3) targeting policy to local employment sectors and investing in quality jobs; and 4) being inclusive.*

Overview

As part of this *OECD Review on Local Job Creation* policies, in-depth fieldwork and research was undertaken to assess local employment and economic development practices using a dashboard methodology developed by the OECD. The dashboard is divided in four thematic areas of analysis, which look at a range of policy and programme indicators to understand implementation practices on the ground. A value of 1 (low) to 5 (high) is assigned to each indicator based on the strengths and weaknesses of the policy approach. In this chapter, each of the four thematic areas of the study is presented and discussed sequentially, accompanied by an explanation of the results. The full results of the OECD Local Job Creation dashboard in Turkey are presented in Figure 3.1 below. For further information on the overall scores as well as the local job creation dashboard, please see the reader's guide at the beginning of this publication.

Figure 3.1. **OECD Reviews on Local Job Creation – Dashboard results for Turkey**

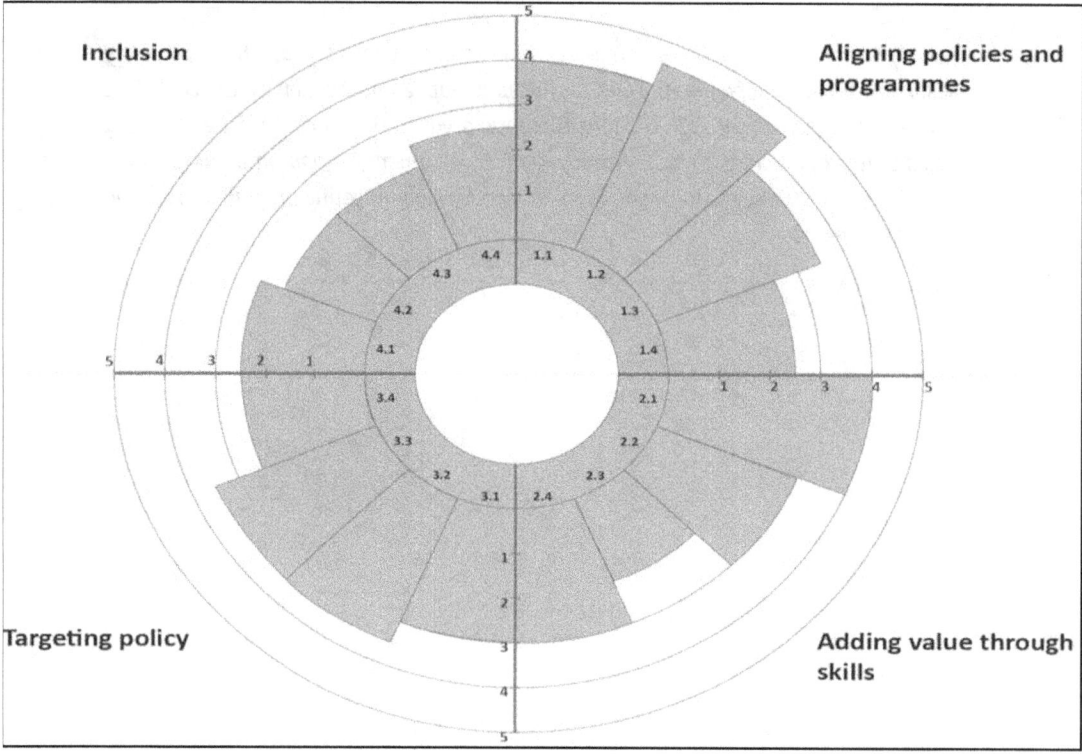

Looking at the overall results from the dashboard exercise, aligning programmes and policies to local economic development needs emerges as an area of policy strength. There appear to be strong governance structures in place in both Trabzon and Kocaeli to guide local employment and economic development policies. However, more needs to be done to align skills development programmes with employer needs, to ensure that policies target higher value added sectors, and to make sure that both policies and programmes focus on tackling disadvantages and building inclusive growth. Each of the thematic results will be described in detail in this chapter with relevant best practices and policy innovations highlighted for future learning in Turkey.

Aligning policies and programmes to local economic development

Figure 3.2. **OECD Dashboard Results for better aligning programmes and policies to local economic development in Turkey**

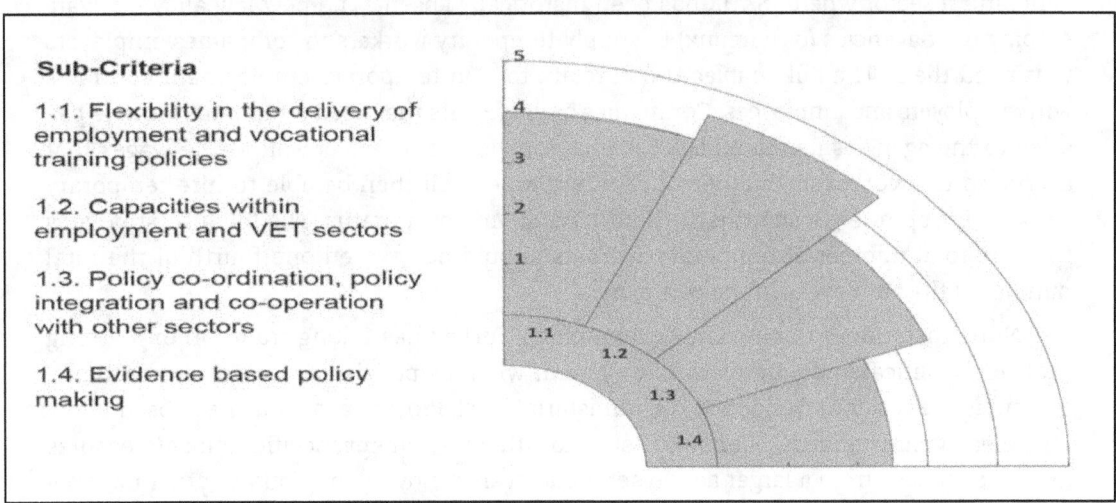

Flexibility in the delivery of employment and vocational training policies

Flexibility is an important element to better align policy and programmes to the changing needs of local labour markets. Flexibility refers to "the possibility to adjust policy at its various design, implementation and delivery stages to make it better adapted to local contexts, actions carried out by other organisations, strategies being pursued, and challenges and opportunities faced" (Giguère and Froy, 2009). Thus, flexibility within this report refers to a characteristic of the administration in charge of the employment and training system and of the policy development process, rather than to a feature of the labour market itself. In this sub-chapter, flexibility of local Public Employment Services (PES) offices and flexibility in local provision of VET are considered separately.

A pre-condition for the achievement of flexibility at the local level is the central government's willingness to delegate certain tasks and responsibilities in different fields to local actors. These may vary from the design of local labour market policies and programmes to deciding on performance targets or on the eligibility conditions for local beneficiaries to take part in the programmes; as well as from the local management of budgets to the outsourcing of services.

Enacted in 2003, the law No. 4904 establishing İŞKUR (an institution set up to continue the work assigned to the dissolved IIBK – the public employment agency serving as a monopoly since the 1930s) represented an important step in this direction. The law enabled İŞKUR to better penetrate local labour markets, as the law stipulated the creation of a larger network of provincial İŞKUR directorates, as opposed to the previously existing network of regional directorates. It also allowed for the establishment and operation of private employment agencies (or bureaux) alongside İŞKUR to supply labour matching services. Even though the law allowed the bureaux to charge fees for helping employers find employees and job seekers find jobs, the role these private companies played in labour markets remained largely limited to the provision of matching services, as Turkish Labour Law did not recognise the temporary worker status until recently.

The most recent bill (no. 1/597) enacted by the General Assembly of the Turkish parliament in May 2016 represents an important change in this regard, and may have serious implications for local and sectoral labour markets in Turkey, including the agricultural sector where İŞKUR has been historically absent. The new law allows private employment agencies (or bureaux) to supply temporary workers to companies/employers that need them. The bill enables the bureaux to sign temporary employment contracts with employers and employees. Companies or employers that need temporary workers pay a fee to the agencies (bureaux) in exchange for their services, as well as the wages that accrue to the worker for his/her work. Companies will then be able to hire temporary workers for up to eight months without having employer status. The bill also stipulates that the total number of temporary workers should not exceed one-fourth of the total number of the employees in the company.

Notwithstanding this recent development, Turkey has a long tradition of a strong centralist political and administrative system, whereby policies and associated actions/measures are typically decided at the ministerial level. Provincial agents are subsequently informed of ministerial decisions and asked to either implement specific actions/measures locally, or choose from a larger action set made available by the ministry or other national body.

Flexibility in the delivery of employment services

Local PES (İŞKUR) offices have some latitude in the implementation of local employment policies although both processes are controlled, by and large, by the central government in Turkey – the Ministry of Labour and the General Directorate of İŞKUR.

Even though they can occasionally design additional initiatives, local İŞKUR offices typically select from an array of nationally designed programmes to serve local needs. Provincial İŞKUR directors in both Kocaeli and Trabzon noted that additional funding for local needs, particularly labour market programmes (LMPs), can usually be obtained from the national headquarters relatively quickly and easily, when local performance targets have been or are likely to be achieved. Set centrally with some input from local branches, these targets may include both inputs and procedures such as the number of training courses given, and take up rates such as the number of people completing certain training courses. Extra funding can be made available for such activities as new course offerings or trainings, if the request sent to the headquarters is well-composed, clearly justifying the need.

Despite the relative flexibility in getting additional funding for labour market programmes as well as in moving the funds allocated to these programmes from one labour market programme to another, provincial directorates are not allowed to transfer funds across different budget lines. In other words, there is some latitude in reallocating funds to different items within a budget line, but no flexibility to do so across budget lines.

Provincial directorates have some influence on decisions regarding outsourcing. They can, for example, weigh in with what to outsource and who to outsource to, unless the labour market programmes in question require that training courses be offered in conjunction with the Ministry of Education, leaving no discretion for local İŞKUR directors. While there are such labour market programmes where service delivery organisations are selected centrally, others can be outsourced to private companies that offer training packages. Local İŞKUR offices can decide which company to outsource these packages to, but companies receiving outsourced service contracts have to work with limited flexibility themselves, as they are given strict targets in terms of the types of people eligible to benefit from their services and the types of services to be provided.

Eligibility criteria for most subsidised training programmes – outsourced or not – are decided nationally, with local stakeholders occasionally consulted through the Provincial Employment and Vocational Training Boards (PEVTBs). For other programmes, local offices can determine the target groups for their subsidised training programmes within broad eligibility criteria. In some cases, local offices can also ask for eligibility regulations to be waived due to circumstantial needs (e.g. strong/urgent need or innovative approach planned), providing some flexibility.

OECD Survey looking at level of local flexibility in employment services

As part of this study, the OECD distributed a questionnaire to local employment offices regarding how they contribute to job creation efforts at the local level. Figure 3.3 shows the percentage of local offices who indicated that they had medium and high local flexibility in the management of employment programmes. 68% of local employments offices reported having relatively high flexibility in choosing target groups and more than half affirmed having medium or high flexibility in performance management. In contrast, few local offices (27.5%) considered they enjoy flexibility in terms of taking a strategic approach to job creation.

Figure 3.3. **Percentage of PES offices reporting medium to high flexibility in the management of programmes and policies, 2014**

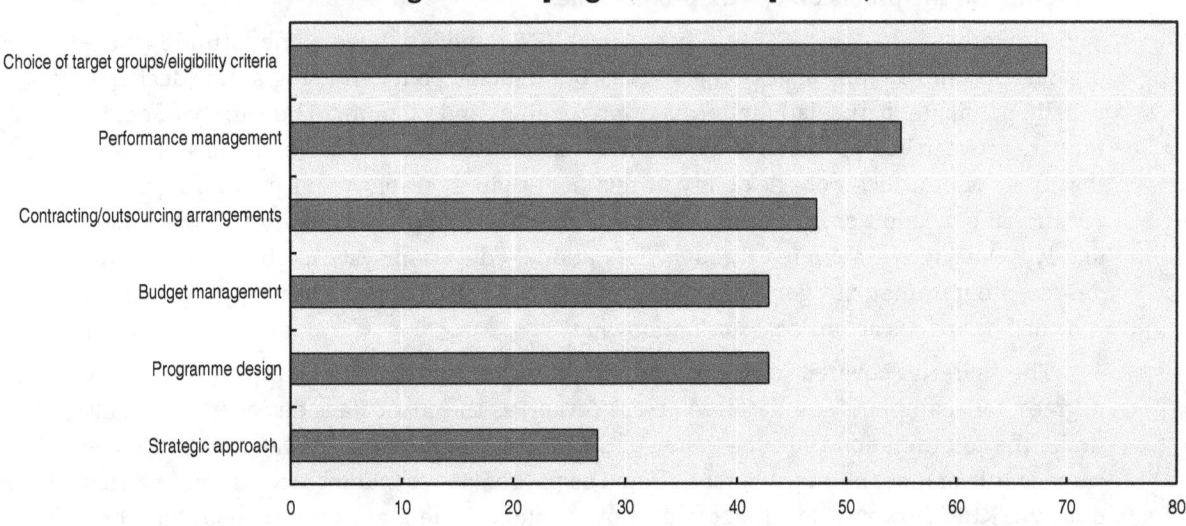

Figure 3.4 shows the percentage of local employment offices which favoured more flexibility in different areas of employment programme management so as to better respond to local labour market conditions. Control over eligibility criteria was identified as the priority area in which to increase flexibility, before performance and budget management, outsourcing arrangements, programme design and strategic approach. Interestingly, while local employment offices report medium-high flexibility in this area, it appears that even more flexibility is preferred when deciding on eligibility criteria and targeting of programmes to certain groups. These results should be interpreted with caution as they are perception-based results based on the interests of local employment offices. However, they are useful in providing a picture of where local employment offices understand they could be more effective in responding to local labour market conditions.

Figure 3.4. **Percentage of PES offices reporting more flexibility would be useful in order to respond to local labour market conditions, 2014**

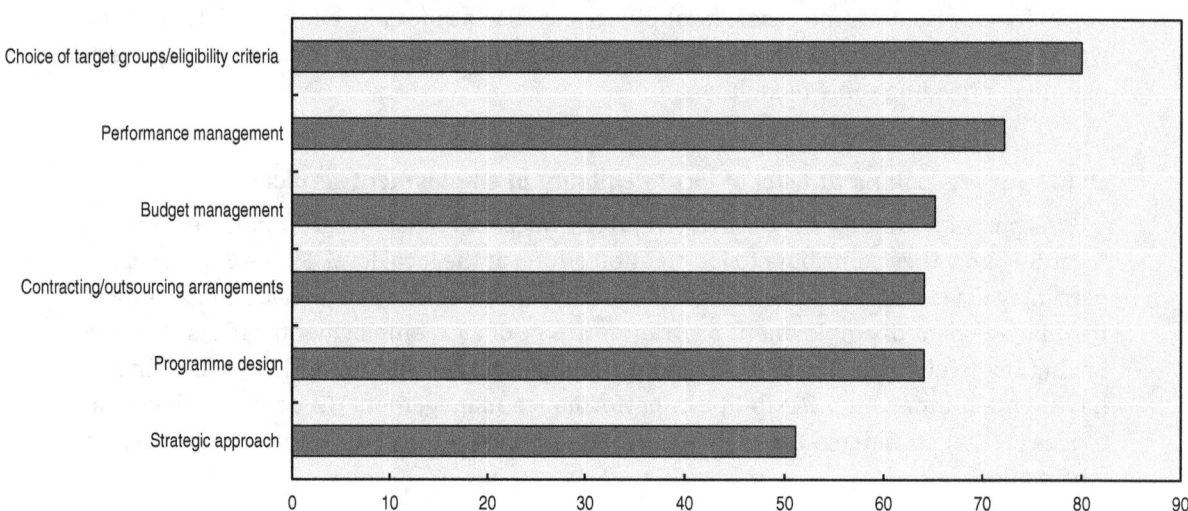

Flexibility in the provision of VET programmes

Similarly to the local İŞKUR offices, local VET providers have some latitude in the organisation and offering of VET programmes, but national policy and programme decisions usually dominate, particularly in terms of preparation and planning. The variety of actors that are active in VET provision and the somewhat less centralised nature of this area mean that there is probably more flexibility in this field than in employment policy. In general, vocational education programmes leading to lower- and upper-secondary (middle school and lycée) degrees are offered through the national education system. These educational degree programmes are generally less flexible than vocational training programmes provided by various actors locally or nationwide.

The material covered in vocational education programmes leading to secondary degrees, for example, is standardised across Turkey, as the curricula is designed nationally under the co-ordination and supervision of the Ministry of National Education (MoNE). The same is true of most training courses offered as part of labour market programmes carried out by İŞKUR. However, local actors and other stakeholders are often consulted when curricula is designed nationally. Local schools and training institutions can also select from a broad set of curricula after deciding which educational or training programmes to offer locally. Sometimes local stakeholders can request special training programmes to meet local needs; the approval process for this is usually completed in a timely fashion.

There are centralised and flexible elements in the planning of vocational and adult training programmes to be provided in the future, depending on the type of programme. While the planning process for some of the programmes such as new adult training courses to be offered through the MoNE's nationwide network of continuous education centres is largely centralised, future local provision of existing training programmes is usually decided on the basis of past local adoption of courses, an analysis of the local economic context or in consultation with other local and regional stakeholders.

Capacities within employment and VET sectors

In both Kocaeli and Trabzon, local VET officials and the İŞKUR directors appeared to be generally satisfied with the amount of financial and human resources available. They noted, however, that more resources could improve labour market outcomes. According to VET officials interviewed for this OECD study and the İŞKUR director in Trabzon, financial resources are fully sufficient for delivering on the established objectives, with some additional capacity to fund ad hoc, new initiatives where needed. The İŞKUR director in Kocaeli, on the other hand, agreed that there is enough funding for delivering on basic objectives but noted that resources for innovative initiatives are limited.

There was a difference of opinion between VET and PES officials concerning the sufficiency of human resources. The Trabzon İŞKUR director considered that his staff size was adequate for the current workload but that more staff would help make the work of the agency more effective. While agreeing with the adequacy of staff size for delivering current objectives, VET officials noted that they had difficulty allocating time to innovative initiatives. The Kocaeli İŞKUR director, on the other hand, highlighted that his staff size was hardly sufficient for implementing the current workload effectively. Both PES officials in Trabzon and Kocaeli agreed that skills levels of the staff were adequate, although there was room for improvement to make the work of the agency fully effective. VET officials in both provinces were also fully satisfied with the skills of their staff.

Provincial İŞKUR offices do regularly share information about developments in the local labour markets (and hence, their performance) with other local stakeholders at Provincial Board of Employment and Vocational Education (PEVTB) meetings.

OECD questionnaire on local capacities in the implementation of policies

When surveying local employment offices across Turkey through an OECD questionnaire, most local offices (69%) indicated having fully sufficient resources to conduct their activities. The main issue was the lack of human resources, with over half of local offices describing them as insufficient. In contrast, labour market knowledge and the skills levels of employees were identified as adequate or better in 87% and 96% of the offices, respectively (see Figure 3.5).

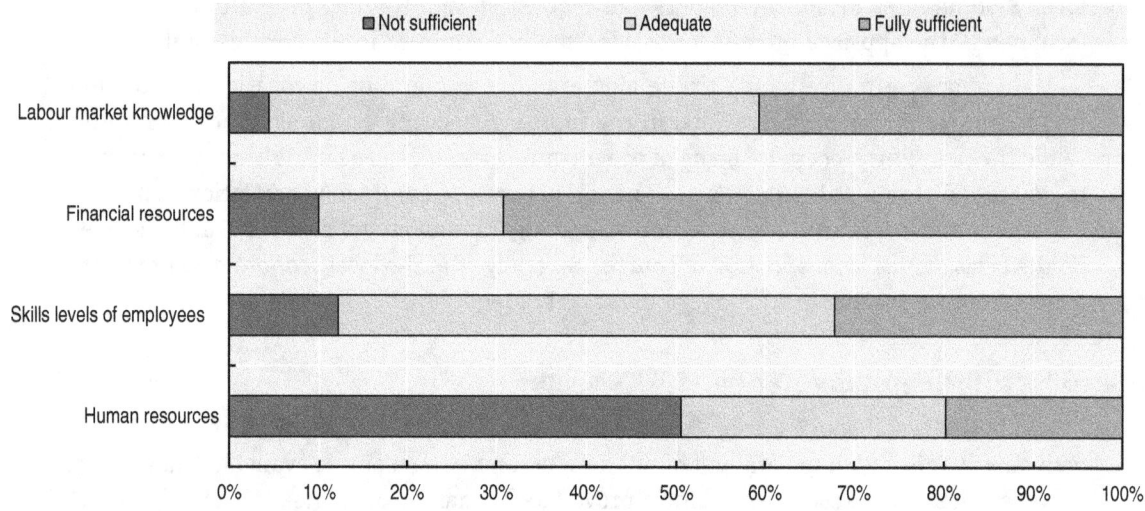

Figure 3.5. **Adequacy of resources at local PES offices, 2014**

Policy co-ordination, policy integration and co-operation with other sectors

There is regular dialogue to explore the possibility of co-operation between various stakeholders *within* and *across* employment and VET policy circles. In addition to monthly executive meetings, there is regular communication between local stakeholders in both employment and VET fields through the quarterly meetings of the Provincial Board of Employment and Vocational Education (PEVTB).[1]

Created to serve as a platform for stakeholder engagement in VET and lifelong learning fields, PEVTBs facilitate the establishment of partnerships with the private sector. They allow various stakeholders to assess general VET needs, particularly with respect to active labour market programmes developed to improve the skills levels of workers, jobseekers and disadvantaged individuals. As such, PEVTBs are useful instruments for local dialogue and collaboration, with the potential to produce solutions for local problems by mobilising resources to increase employment and reduce skills gaps.

At the provincial level, PEVTBs bring together representatives from multiple agencies and associations, including those coming from districts or townships within the province. Turkish law lists PEVTB members as follows: Mayors from local municipalities (metropolitan mayor and district mayors); Provincial directors of the Ministries of Education, Industry, Trade, Science and Technology, and Customs and Commerce; representatives of local chambers of trade and industry, local branches of the confederation of the employer unions, and the confederation of the tradesmen' and artisans' associations; local representatives of trade unions; representatives of other associations, NGOs and special interest groups such as the disabled; and one local academic.

PEVTBs meet quarterly to decide on employment policies and strategies, prepare local action plans and monitor their implementation. A sub-committee produces the action plans for the implementation of the decisions and determines the party(/ies) in charge. Secretariat duties are carried out jointly by the Provincial İŞKUR Directorate and the Provincial Directorate of the MoNE. The Executive Committee follows up on the decisions taken and surveys the local labour market. Nevertheless, when a PEVTB decides that new kinds of vocational courses need to be offered, the final decision making body is İŞKUR's General Directorate.

While PEVTB's in Kocaeli and Trabzon regularly meet in provincial centres, they discuss the employment and skills issues faced not only by stakeholders in the provincial centre but also in different towns and districts across the province. They are, in other words, in charge of identifying, monitoring and formulating VET solutions to meet the skills needs of *local* labour markets and to prevent employment losses in all districts/ townships. After the establishment of Regional Development Agencies in the late 2000s, these agencies joined the other bodies represented in the PEVTBs.

Collaboration within public employment services

Nearly all local employment offices collaborate with local public institutions, trade associations, universities, colleges and public training centres. Specifically, close to half of them collaborate with local public institutions and trade associations. However, collaboration between non-government organisations working with foreigners and private employment agencies is relatively limited.

Looking at the results of the OECD questionnaire to local employment offices, outreach to employers is widespread, with 94.5% of local offices reporting active efforts in this area. More than two thirds of local offices stated that training is geared towards meeting employer demands. Other than that, local employment offices indicated that only 16.5% of employers report problems with training curricula not being aligned to their needs.

Figure 3.6 shows the activities that local employment offices undertake as part of their local employment and economic development programmes. Local employment offices appear to be very active, particularly in relation to placing unemployed individuals into local job opportunities (all offices), promoting apprenticeships and other work-based training opportunities (97.5%) and informing employers of labour market regulation and employment promotion (94.5%).

Figure 3.6. **Percentage of PES offices conducting specific activities as part of local employment and economic development programmes**

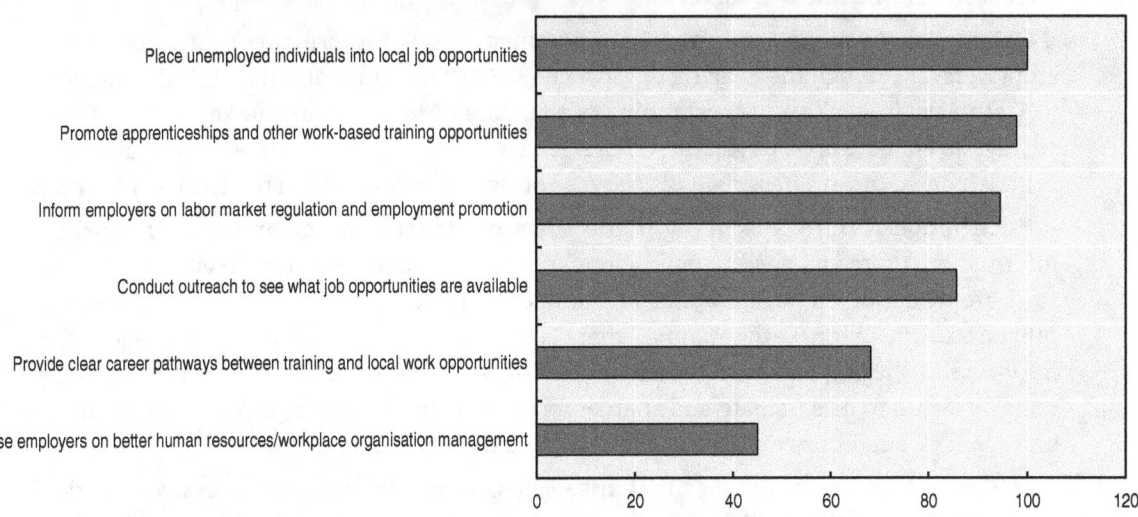

Collaboration with the private sector and area-based partnerships at local level

PEVTBs' regular members include representatives of local chambers of trade and industry, local branches of the confederation of employer unions, and the confederation of the tradesmens' and artisans' associations. This allows private sector organisations to directly contribute to the decision making process regarding employment and training policies.

A notable example of collaboration with the private sector was the UMEM (or Specialised Occupational Development Centres) project, which was introduced in 2010 but ended in 2016. Unemployed people registered with İŞKUR were able to enrol in these courses (extended to also cover agricultural and service sectors in 2012) free of charge. They further received a pre-determined amount for their per diem expenses and were provided health and accident insurance coverage during the training period.

Local chambers of commerce/industry played a key role in this project by identifying local employers with skills shortages or skills needs in specific areas. The UMEM project created its own governance model. Rather than relying on PEVTBs as the decision-making forum, UMEM created "Provincial Course Management Boards". Sitting on these boards were local representatives of the project partners: the Provincial Directors of İŞKUR and the MoNE, along with principals of vocational high schools that serve as project training centres in the province and the secretary general of the local chamber of industry, who is typically the chairperson of the board.

Evidence based policy making

Evidence-based policy-making has not been traditionally widespread in Turkey. Nonetheless, recent efforts have been made to encourage such practices, which can influence the way that employment and skills policies are being designed and implemented at the local or provincial levels.

Since 2007, İŞKUR has been conducting research on the labour market demand for jobs. Data and information is collected in co-operation with Turkstat (through a partnership established in 2011), which feeds into the planning of active labour market programmes and policies. Most of this information is collected at the provincial level, given that there are availability issues regarding jobs and occupational data at the district level (the administrative level below the provinces in Turkey).

Some labour market information is obtained through informal conversations with employers, or through the analysis of vacancies. PEVTB meetings also help İŞKUR and local VET officials develop an understanding of the state of local labour markets. While local surveys on employers' skills gaps and shortages are undertaken, such surveys are usually not complemented by an assessment of the types of skills available within the local workforce.

Although progress is being made towards developing strong labour market information, there is a need to build more knowledge-exchange among regions in Turkey to share evidence on "what works". A number of regions in Turkey are implementing programmes in an innovative manner; there is therefore an opportunity to encourage more information sharing on these successful practices. At the national level, more could be done by İŞKUR to disseminate and share information among regions through conferences and capacity building activities which promote these types of activities.

Where there are joint issues that arise across local administrative areas, authorities tend to co-ordinate under the supervision of the provincial governor's office. Local bodies collaborate with the aim of responding to developments in local labour markets and training needs in different districts or townships within each province. There is a certain degree of inter-provincial co-ordination as well, notably thanks to regional plans. The administrative areas of many Regional Development Agencies (RDAs) often cover more than one province.

MARKA, East Marmara Regional Development Agency, for example, includes the provinces of Bolu, Duzce, Sakarya and Yalova alongside Kocaeli. Likewise, the area covered by DOKA, the Eastern Black Sea Regional Development Agency, includes 6 provinces: Artvin, Giresun, Gumushane, Ordu, Rize and Trabzon. Regional development strategies designed by relevant RDAs necessarily require some joint work and co-ordination.

Adding value through skills

Figure 3.7. **OECD Dashboard Results – Adding Value through Skills**

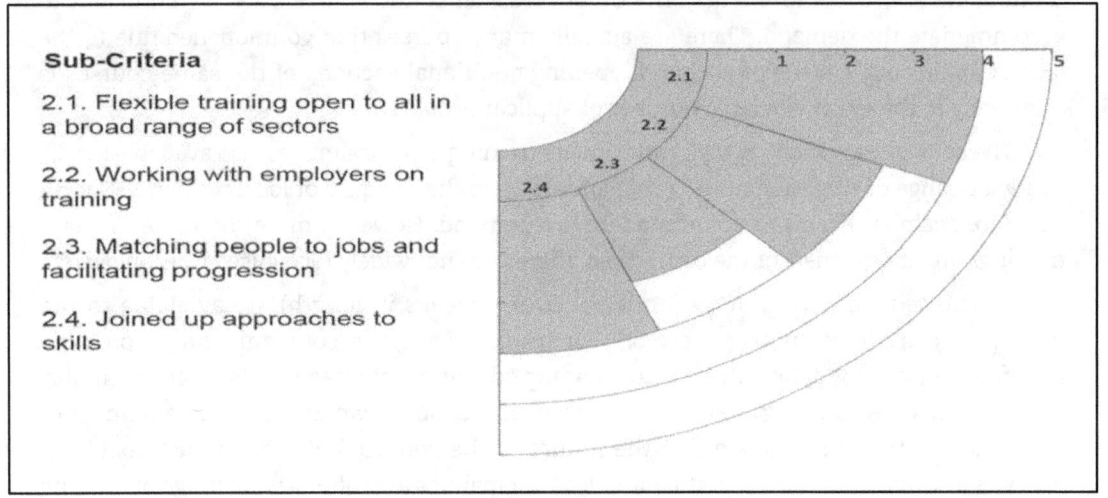

Flexible training open to all in a broad range of sectors

While priority sectors vary across regions, implying different skills development needs for different regions, all strategy documents and action plans related to unemployment or skills mismatch commonly emphasise the need to strengthen the VET system. Many of these policy analyses also converge on the primary areas of concern, namely facilitating *school-to-work transition* for students seeking (secondary or tertiary) vocational school degrees, expanding the *capacity* of the VET system and improving *access* to VET programs. The latest Vocational and Technical Education Strategy Document and the Action Plan covering the period from 2014 to 2018 are also structured along these axes.

A number of issues with the VET system in Turkey have been identified, such as enhancing the capabilities of teachers/trainers, developing new curricula in partnership with the private sector and improving the physical infrastructure of VET schools and institutes. Structuring the national qualifications system so as to create a well-functioning vocational qualifications system has also been a major challenge in Turkey. There have been some attempts to improve quality assurance, including the establishment of a vocational qualifications authority (VQA) through the Turkish National Qualifications Authority (NQA) in 2006. This new body is responsible for evaluating qualifications acquired through all VET programmes (formal and non-formal) in order to facilitate the awarding of national certificates. However, a number of other issues remain unresolved.

The current lack of an integrated system to recognise skills irrespective of the nature of the institution where they are acquired (e.g. whether formal or informal) creates inefficiencies and inhibits skills transfer. In general, skills acquired through prior informal learning are not treated equally to those acquired via formal education, which restricts mobility between formal and non-formal frameworks. This feeds into the already existing perception that VET degrees are of lesser value than regular high school degrees or bachelor's degrees obtained from universities.

In Kocaeli and Trabzon, the range of trainings offered at the local level is fairly diverse, but some students (particularly those living in smaller districts or townships) may be forced to travel or commute to the provincial centre to take certain courses. Flexible short-term modular training at the local level is available in a wide variety of subject areas or sectors. During the OECD study visit, officials also indicated that courses available for both types of training are affordable to the majority of local residents and course sizes are sufficient to accommodate the demand. There are actually many courses that go unopened due to the lack of applicants. On the other hand, opening additional sections of the same courses is often easy in the event of a large number of applicants.

The same observations apply to after-hours training. Such training is also available locally in a wide range of subject areas at a cost affordable to the majority of local residents. Course sizes are again sufficient to accommodate the demand. However, more than 75% of these trainings are not certified, or the certificates offered are not widely recognised by employers.

Subsidised training courses (under or over 6 weeks in length) are available to the unemployed in a large number of sectors. For employed workers, companies are responsible for offering training opportunities. Local adult education centres (HEMs in Turkish) also provide subsidised trainings to the unemployed and to active workers in a large number of areas. Eligibility criteria depend on the nature of the courses but are kept as flexible as possible in order to encourage participation. Municipalities also offer a wide range of training courses that are practically open to everyone.

As far as VET courses are concerned, such courses may cover basic skills, but also higher-level generic skills such as networking, communication, leadership, innovation and entrepreneurship. During the OECD study visit, VET, adult training and PES officials commonly stated that subsidised occupational training programmes, adult training and basic skills training programmes meet demand in both Kocaeli and Trabzon.

Working with employers on training

VET officials and employers reported that training curricula are not well aligned to employer needs, leading to additional company-financed workplace training being provided to workers. Larger companies tend to fund more training programmes (see Box 3.1) in a wider range of areas for their employees. In contrast, smaller companies tend to keep workplace training to a minimum, often without offering any training courses to their employees other than those required by law (such as workplace safety trainings).

The representative of TİSK – the confederation of employers' unions – in Kocaeli estimated that their member companies invest, on average, between 0.5-1% of payroll in workforce training and skills development, while the estimated figure in Trabzon amounts to 1-3%. Even though only larger companies become members of the employers' unions, 0.5% of the payroll often represents a small amount of funding. Furthermore, the estimated ratio of training expenses to payroll may also include trainings received by engineers, which are particularly expensive. VET and PES officials in Trabzon and Kocaeli report lobbying from public sector actors to try to increase workplace training efforts by local companies. There are also specific programmes and initiatives such as the UMEM project that include workplace training as a critical component (see Box 3.2).

> **Box 3.1. Employment-guaranteed training courses for aircraft mechanics in Kocaeli**
>
> In light of forecasts pointing to a rapidly growing global demand for aircraft mechanics from airline and aviation industries, Kocaeli University's Faculty of Aviation and Aeronautics, Turkish Airlines Technic Inc., and İŞKUR have collaborated to offer vocational courses to train assistant aircraft maintenance mechanics to meet the growing need for employees in aircraft maintenance. Around 500 of the trainees who have graduated from 2012 to date were immediately employed by Turkish Airlines.
>
> The course lasts for six months and is taught by Kocaeli University's faculty members. Trainees are admitted into the programme based on their performance in a written exam and an interview. The course content is determined according to the needs of Turkish Airlines. Modules on aircraft engine and aircraft body maintenance are available. The courses are in the 50% Employment Guarantee category: Turkish Airlines guarantees to employ 50% of the trainees upon successful completion of the training program. Nevertheless, the actual employment rate of graduates, currently standing at 90%, is much higher.
>
> *Source:* Interviews with İŞKUR representatives.

> **Box 3.2. UMEM project**
>
> The UMEM (or Specialised Occupational Development Centres) project is a nationwide vocational training initiative introduced to address skills mismatch in Turkey. The labour market was previously in a state where hundreds of thousands of low- or unskilled individuals remained unemployed, while large numbers of vacancies went unfilled due to a lack of qualified or skilled applicants.
>
> Also known as Skills'10, the UMEM project (which has now ended) was carried out nationally by a joint public-private-academia consortium made up of İŞKUR, the Ministry of Labour and Social Security, the Ministry of National Education, the Turkish Union of the Chambers and Exchanges (TOBB) and TOBB University of Economics and Technology. When the UMEM project was first introduced in 2010, there were about 2.7 million unemployed in the country, while many job openings posted by employers in the manufacturing industry remained unfilled due to a lack of skilled jobseekers. The project aimed to reduce the severity of such skills shortages by allowing the unemployed to acquire the necessary skills through training courses offered in selected public vocational high schools outside regular class hours. For this purpose, about USD100 million was invested initially to improve physical infrastructure and educational facilities at these schools.
>
> The main idea behind the project was to offer training courses specifically designed to endow the unemployed with the skills needed by local employers. When employers facing skills shortages reported them through the local chamber of commerce/industry, İŞKUR announced its intent to offer relevant courses. In addition, the unemployed registering in the course received an allowance to cover their per diem expenses, and had health and accident insurance coverage during the training period. The whole project was funded by İŞKUR. The programme combined theoretical, in-class training and workplace training – typically at plants/establishments whose reported skills shortages were meant to be filled by the graduates of the training course in question – allowing them to be seriously considered for employment at the same company. If a trainee was employed after the successful completion of both the in-class and workplace components of the training, the

> **Box 3.2. UMEM project** *(cont.)*
>
> company that employed her/him enjoyed additional tax and social security premium breaks (for a longer period of time if the trainee employed was younger than 29 or female).
>
> As a unique example of Public-Private-University partnership, UMEM/Skill'10 project located the private sector at the centre of the vocational training system through the Chambers of Industry and Commerce. The key governance organ for the co-ordination and conduct of training courses in every province was the "Provincial Course Management Board." Created specifically as the governance of the UMEM (Skills '10) project, these boards brought together local representatives of the project partners: the Provincial Directors of İŞKUR and the MoNE, along with principals of vocational high schools that served as project training centres in the province and the secretary general of the local chamber of commerce/industry. The latter was typically the chairperson of the board. Demand for workers with the skills most needed by local employers was collected through the local chamber, and the board quickly decided which training courses to open based on this information.
>
> As highlighted in Chapter 1, Building on the experience of the UMEM project, the Vocational Training and Employment Mobilisation Protocol will involve the co-operation between the Turkish Employment Agency (İŞKUR) and the Turkish Union of Chambers and Commodity Exchanges (TOBB) in order to prepare the Turkish labour force for the jobs of the future. The Protocol aims to achieve better employment outcomes for job seekers through organised counselling, training, job placements, and workplace experience opportunities. Under this protocol, in addition to İŞKUR's provincial directorates and service centres, the number of "İŞKUR Service Points" will be increased to provide greater outreach opportunities.
>
> *Source:* Interviews with İŞKUR representatives.

Dual training and apprenticeships

Formal VET programmes in Turkey have two pillars: theoretical and practical (in-company) training. Students attending vocational and technical high schools must complete part of their in-company training through internships totalling 300 hours. They can finalise at most one-third of the required internship by the end of the 10th grade, leaving the rest to the period after the 11th grade. Students can fulfil internship requirements during weekends, or semester and summer breaks but once they reach the 12th grade, vocational education itself is provided in enterprises three days a week (ETF, 2015).

In addition, there are apprenticeship schools where practical training provided in enterprises is combined with theoretical training provided in vocational education centres. When the MoNE was restructured in 2011, several departments in charge of formal vocational education were merged into the General Directorate for Vocational and Technical Education, while the General Directorate for Apprenticeship and Non-Formal Education was restructured as the General Directorate for Life-Long Learning (LLL). The General Directorate for LLL is now in charge of non-formal education, including the so-called "Public Education Centres" offering various continuing education (vocational and otherwise) programmes to people older than 17 years, as well as apprenticeship training (World Bank, 2014). The country's new LLL strategy stresses the need to improve access to lifelong learning beyond the formal education system, including learning in enterprises. Within this context, the apprenticeship system can be seen as an important channel to facilitate school-to-work transition. The strategy places special emphasis on the link between better education outcomes and better employment outcomes for young people and women, without overlooking regional disparities (ETF, 2015).

The development of alternative pathways to traditional schooling through open and distance learning or apprenticeship is a priority of the Turkish Sectoral Operational Programme for Employment, Education and Social Policies, covering the period from 2014-20. Within this context, the document attributes special importance to strengthening the apprenticeship system at different levels by adopting a dual approach (school-based and enterprise-based training) (ETF, 2015).

Accordingly, the most recent bill awaiting Parliament approval intends to integrate apprenticeship education into the formal education system. The bill recognises apprenticeship schools as an alternative means of completing compulsory education. It also modifies conditions for entry into an apprenticeship school and requires that entrants have at least a middle school degree (whereas an elementary school degree currently suffices). The bill also envisages that enterprises employing 10 or more staff provide occupational skills training to at least as many vocational and technical education students as 5% of their staff. Enterprises providing occupational skills training to 10 or more students will also be required to establish a training unit staffed by qualified trainers who are skilled crafts people with pedagogical training.

When enacted, the bill will help improve the quality of apprenticeship education, and potentially increase applications received by apprenticeship centres. Currently, the demand for apprenticeship training is relatively low, even though there is considerable diversity in the subject areas of such training. During the OECD study visit, VET officials in both Kocaeli and Trabzon indicated that apprenticeship training is offered in a large variety of subject areas, including in the services sector. However, such types of training are taken up by less than 20% of young people aged 15-24 years old. By contrast, the availability of customised training is quite limited, although new tailored training courses can be developed relatively quickly (i.e. within three months or less). VET and PES officials indicated that less than 25% of customised training is certified. While there is no particular support to stimulate skills development in SMEs other than some *ad hoc* adaption of existing training programmes, employers' associations help pool funds for training.

Matching people to jobs and facilitating progression

In addition to helping shape national labour market policies that contribute to job creation, İŞKUR's main responsibilities include the supply of job matching services (and overseeing similar activities of private employment agencies/bureaux) as well as the provision of information, guidance and counselling services to students, job seekers and employers on skills training programmes, qualifications and occupations/careers.

İŞKUR has recently made significant efforts to hire job and vocational counsellors with the aim of guiding local job seekers, including youth, into suitable positions or training programmes that best fit their skills and aspirations. Job and Vocational Counselling staff regularly organise school visits to provide careers advice to local youth. Job and vocational counsellors work at Career Information Centres created at provincial directorates and local service centres. They provide guidance and advice to students, parents, job seekers, school counsellors, teachers and principals; or anyone seeking jobs or training programmes, individually or in groups. They also make workplace visits to stay in touch with employers and to stay informed about their openings and skill needs. As a result of these activities, counsellors are well informed about local labour markets. Table 3.1 presents some data on İŞKUR's nationwide counselling activities.

Table 3.1. **İŞKUR Career and Job Counselling Services, 2010-14**

Year	Individual interviews		Number of students served at school visits	Number of parents conferences held
	Career counselling	Job counselling		
2010	3 649	16 075	53 795	-
2011	4 504	160 607	58 675	-
2012	36 236	805 257	277 393	37
2013	47 845	1 585 005	632 299	131
2014	69 578	2 494 762	981 238	95

Source: İŞKUR (2016a).

Both employed and unemployed adults also have access to career advice through İŞKUR. During the OECD study visit, PES and VET officials in both Kocaeli and Trabzon noted that graduates from various types of adult and youth training programmes are linked to local industries through local career fairs and other activities, which İŞKUR career advisors help to organise (see Box 3.3). However, there is no systematic support for the professional development of less-qualified employees, nor is there a policy focus on encouraging their career progression.

Box 3.3. **Local Job Fairs: Collaboration in Job-Matching Services**

An exemplary İŞKUR initiative is the organisation of local job fairs held with the participation of local employers, universities and schools. Fairs are organised regularly in both Kocaeli and Trabzon by the İŞKUR provincial directorates. They offer a forum where parties searching for jobs or employees are brought together.

Fairs help raise awareness about vacant positions, internship possibilities and skills shortages in local job markets; they facilitate the application of interested participants, and act as platforms for universities, schools and the private sector to meet. Fairs also allow young people to benefit from career guidance services – they receive advice choosing appropriate career paths and ease the school-to-work transition by laying out employers' expectations and requirements. Such events provide a solid basis for larger and perhaps more comprehensive future collaborations between the stakeholders in employment.

Source: Trabzon İstihdam Fuarı; Kocaeli Doğu Marmara İstihdam Fuarı, 2015.

Activation and job matching services

While the unemployed can benefit from career advice provided by İŞKUR, there is no systematic counselling specifically designed to help the recently unemployed back into work. Online job matching services are available, which people can access from home by using their e-government identification details. While job seekers can use this online service and other job matching services provided by local İŞKUR offices, some sectors or employers experience difficulties accessing skilled people. Companies that seek well educated, highly skilled professionals often need to turn to privately operated job matching services. For others, graduates of training programmes like the UMEM project can be contacted through local İŞKUR offices. There is no incentive for ensuring the sustainability of job matches and there is no follow up by PES staff to ensure job retention, except for people completing training courses that guarantee placement in a job.

Integrated local approaches to skills

There appears to be a lack of awareness among economic development organisations of the need to retain and attract talent. During the OECD study visit, greater attention to such issues was given at the Metropolitan Mayor's office in Kocaeli and at the Regional Development Agency office in Trabzon.

While local strategies/policies may mention the importance of retaining and attracting talent, no specific actions have been taken in this field. In Trabzon, for example, the Economic Development Agency is trying to attract foreign investment (particularly from the Gulf) towards the tourism industry. Given the general lack of interest among the local workforce to take on jobs in this industry, local stakeholders have identified the need to attract skilled individuals from outside the region to fill vacancies in the tourism sector. Yet, no policy initiative has been developed to tackle this issue.

Additionally, there is no evidence of the existence of integrated approaches to skills that bring together local actors working on two or more of the following areas: skills supply and development, management of local skills and talent flows (attracting and retaining talent), integration of low-skilled individuals into the labour market and career advice for the young. The major exception in both provinces was the UMEM courses which, by design, require that provincial İŞKUR office works closely with the local chamber(s), provincial education authorities and school principals.

Targeting policies to local employment sectors and investing in quality jobs

Figure 3.8. **OECD Dashboard results – targeting policies to local employment sectors and investing in quality jobs**

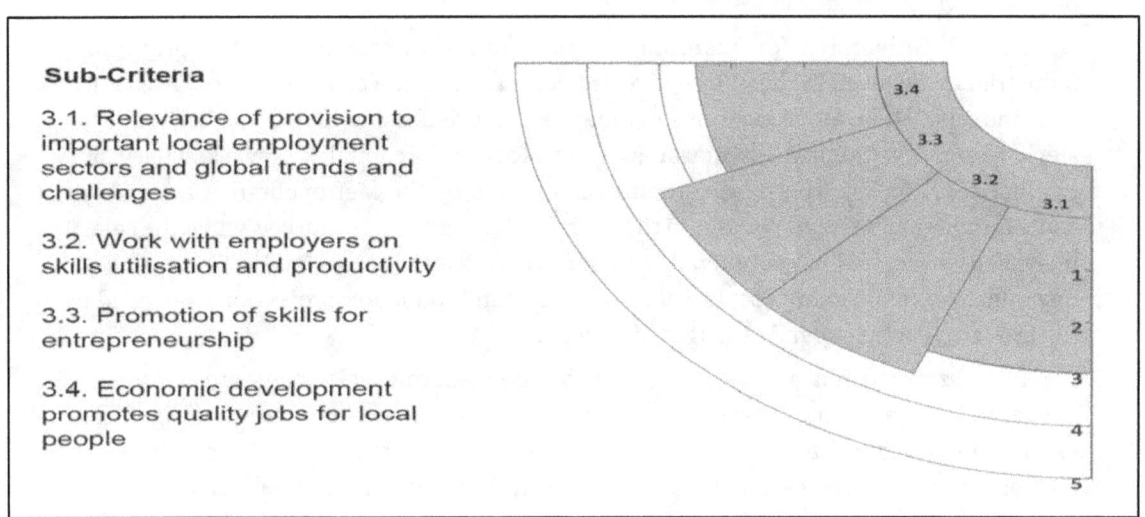

Relevance of skills provision to local employment sectors

Regional development agencies list the leading sectors in terms of employment in Kocaeli and Trabzon. According to MARKA, the Eastern Marmara Development Agency, the current leaders of sectoral employment in Kocaeli are the metal industry, construction, transportation and logistics, chemicals, and automotive and parts. The leading employer in Trabzon is agriculture, including hazelnuts and tea as well as fisheries. DOKA, the Eastern Black Sea Development Agency, indicates that the leading manufacturing activities are food and beverages, as well as construction products. Tourism is an emerging area of employment.

In terms of development visions, both provinces have identified priority sectors for local development through provincial development board meetings and similar forums attended by local stakeholders as well as through vision development/foresight exercises of the local Chambers of Industry. It is not clear, however, whether there are systematic action plans or a formal assignment of roles to local stakeholders to ensure the development of priority sectors. It is also unclear whether the skills and education levels of the *existing* labour force in the provinces match the desired sectors of priority, and whether the implications for local labour markets of such sector choices is given sufficient consideration in these exercises.

It seems that neither province debates possible trade-offs between creating "more employment (lower unemployment) with lower quality jobs" versus "less employment (higher unemployment) with higher quality jobs". This issue depends on the choice of priority sectors, as there is an almost unspoken consensus on the desirability of higher value-added sectors. This obviously hints at an implicit preference for higher quality jobs to be brought by the development of priority sectors. However, this may come at the expense of generating fewer jobs for the local workforce, whose skill and education levels may not be compatible with the sectors envisioned to be developed locally.

During the OECD study visit, it was revealed that Kocaeli's vision is to stay (or even move) away from the manufacturing industry towards high-tech and high value-added sectors. Accordingly, the province has long been lobbying the government to become the ICT hub of Turkey, similar to a Silicon Valley in the USA. Kocaeli aims to retain the automotive and parts industry, while promoting an increase in the use of higher-tech production processes within the sector.

Kocaeli University, for example, offers training programmes for programming industrial robots used in the automotive sector and tailors the courses to the needs of the local industry. There are also visions to promote the logistics and tourism sector, and even steps taken by the municipality towards making Kocaeli the capital of movie and television production in Turkey. The movie studios constructed by the Metropolitan Municipality's contributions are being rented out to the booming film industry in Turkey, while the sale of television shows has proven lucrative both at home and abroad. Kocaeli University has responded by establishing vocational courses to train production professionals needed by the industry, such as sound and light technicians.

In Trabzon, there is a strong consensus on the need to develop the tourism industry. This seems like a natural choice given the severe space constraints preventing significant expansion of industrial zones, coupled with the natural beauty of the province and increasing interest and demand from Arab and Iranian tourists. Tourism establishments currently request the most investment incentives from the state. DOKA's SWOT exercises also highlighted transportation and logistics (particularly to Iran and the Caucasus) and the health industry as sectors with strong development potential. Motivated again by the severity of spatial constraints, the local chamber has established a biotechnology sector and examined the possibility of developing other R&D intensive sectors where production activity does not require large amounts of space.

Provincial İŞKUR directors in both provinces admitted that no *formal* analysis is carried out to understand the potential impact of global trends on local labour markets, or to tailor employment or re-skilling programmes to sectors that are leading employers in the provincial or local labour market. Provincial İŞKUR directors and staff occasionally visit local employers and regularly meet employer representatives during PEVTB meetings. Furthermore, as previously mentioned, companies are consulted within the scope of the research looking at labour market demand, which is conducted once annually. The same process is applied to adult education courses. In brief, there are signs of a growing emphasis on certain sectors but these are often not based on systematic and formal analyses.

> **Box 3.4. Outsourcing employment for regional growth: The case of tourism sector in Trabzon**
>
> During the OECD study visit, the potential for employment generation of the tourism sector and the advantages it would yield to the province were discussed with representatives from the Regional Development Agency, DOKA. DOKA picked tourism as a priority sector for local development for a number of reasons. First, topographic and geographic constraints (including shortages of arable land and physical space for industrial development, and the difficulty of land access) largely prevent significant development in the manufacturing and agricultural industries in Trabzon, leaving the service sector as the only promising industry for local development and employment generation.
>
> The recent boom of tourists from Arabic-speaking countries, particularly from the Gulf, makes tourism a likely candidate to boost the development of the service industry in Trabzon. The number of Arab visitors coming to Trabzon, especially for ecological and health tourism purposes, went up from just 30 000 in 2010 to 260 000 in 2014 (DOKA, 2014b). However, some cultural and education-related barriers may lead to difficulties in attracting local workers into the hospitality sector, creating severe skills shortages that are likely to create problems in service quality.
>
> *Source:* Interviews with DOKA representatives and DOKA (2014).

Co-operation with employers to improve skills utilisation and work organisation

Recent OECD data looking at job quality shows that Turkey ranks near the bottom among OECD countries in terms of earning quality, labour market security and quality of the working environment (see Table 3.2). The figure shows Turkey's average ranking out of a group of 34 OECD countries on the three indicators that have been defined in the OECD's job quality framework. In all three cases, Turkey falls among the bottom-third of performers. However, Turkey has improved its position over time in terms of labour market insecurity, moving from 33rd position among OECD countries to 28th.

Table 3.2. **Job quality indicators, Turkey ranking and selected averages**

	Earnings quality (USD PPP)			Labour market insecurity (%)			Job strain (%)		
	2007	2010	2013	2007	2010	2013	2007	2010	2013
Ranking: Turkey	-	32	-	33	29	28	-	23	-
Top-third score average	21.7	24.6	24.4	5.9	11.1	12.5	-	56.5	-
Bottom-third score average	7.7	7.8	7.5	1.6	2.3	2.1	-	33.3	-

Source: OECD (2017).

There are programmes, networks and schemes involving major employers or sector organisations to improve skills utilisation and work organisation. The UMEM project is an example of specific training courses being offered to meet the demand of local employers, who report their skills shortages or skills needs in specific areas. The so-called Course Management Boards for training courses offered within the framework of the UMEM project serve as a co-ordination mechanism between the project partners from public and private sectors: İŞKUR, the Ministry of Education, and the Turkish Union of the Chambers of Industry and Commerce. İŞKUR counsellors also stay in touch with local employers to identify their skill needs through regular visits (see Table 3.3).

Table 3.3. **İŞKUR counsellor visits to workplaces, 2010-14**

Year	Number of workplaces visited	Number of workplace visits	Updated vocational training course portfolios
2010	-	42 025	187
2011	-	70 505	14
2012	-	183 373	0
2013	234 303	376 654	415
2014	281 121	410 734	1 784

Source: İŞKUR (2016b).

A new initiative also provides legal grounds to enable the private sector to fund vocational schools in Organised Industrial Zones. Employers are encouraged to become involved in designing curricula and teacher recruitment; a predetermined amount of public funding is provided for each student enrolled. Representatives of sector bodies such as local chambers of commerce and industry or employers' associations mentioned no strategies adopted or initiatives taken to improve work organisation/labour productivity on a sectoral scale.

Some help is available from local universities that carry out applied research in a limited number of fields that are relevant to the local economy. However, local universities mostly focus on general specialty areas without necessarily keeping an eye on the local economy. The main channel for academia to co-operate with local industry is through technology parks established and operated by local universities. Both Kocaeli University and Karadeniz Technical University have well-developed technology parks where local companies conduct applied research in collaboration with local academics.

Promotion of entrepreneurship skills through training and education

Comprehensive approaches are taken to encourage entrepreneurship through public employment programmes, and specially designed courses are offered as part of the active labour market programmes in both provinces to encourage entrepreneurship. Turkey's self-employment rates are significantly higher than the European average (see Figure 3.9) and the self-employed account for roughly 33% of the country's employment rate (OECD, 2016a). This phenomenon is not necessarily positive, since the measure includes unpaid family workers who tend to cluster around the agriculture and retail sectors. Many of these entrepreneurs are likely to be so-called "'necessity entrepreneurs", who made up 3.2% of Turkey's population in 2010. This distinction is important because, relative to "opportunity entrepreneurs", "necessity entrepreneurs" are seen as less likely to make contributions to innovation systems and to job creation. Indeed, at 1.45 in the year 2010, the ratio of "opportunity" to "necessity" early-stage entrepreneurs in Turkey was quite low – 21st out of 24 countries participating in the Global Entrepreneurship Monitor 2012 study (Karadeniz, 2011).

In line with the prevalence of "necessity entrepreneurs", the gap between the total number of self-employed individuals and the number of self-employed who are in turn employers is much larger in Turkey than in other European countries. In 2015, approximately

Figure 3.9. **Trends in self-employment (%): Turkey and selected OECD countries, 2006-15**

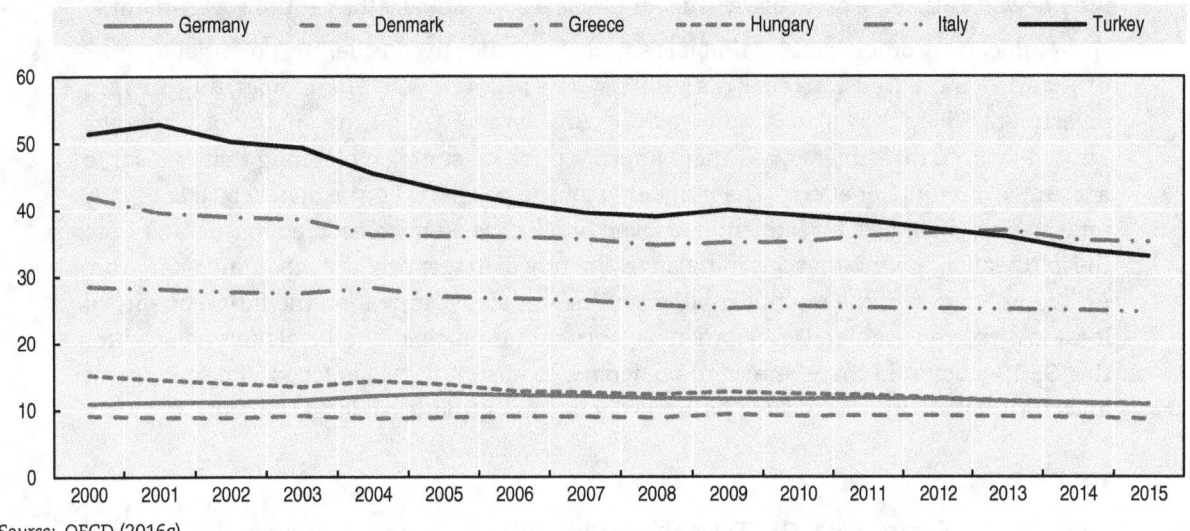

Source: OECD (2016c).

one in five of Turkey's entrepreneurs generated a job for at least another individual. In contrast, almost one in two Hungarian entrepreneurs had registered employees (Eurostat, 2016). This suggests that entrepreneurship has the potential to play a larger role in increasing Turkey's employment rate. However, a mere increase in the funds offered to entrepreneurs may simply favour the rise of "necessity entrepreneurship". In order to reap more of the economic advantages associated with entrepreneurship, training and support in navigating the difficulties individuals find when setting up shop are likely to do more to encourage "opportunity entrepreneurs" at the local level.

In addition, attention should be paid to the role of women in entrepreneurship. Although self-employment accounted for 38% of all female employment in 2015, males are more likely than females to start a new firm in order to exploit a business opportunity. Further, highly educated women usually prefer working for others (Karadeniz, 2011). These patterns point to the precarious position women hold in the Turkish labour market. They also suggest that particular emphasis should be placed both on securing females position in the labour market and on fostering their entrepreneurial spirit. Nonetheless, much of the latter goal may depend on achievements at the primary school level, since it is associated with socially built-in perceptions. Such a logic might also apply to fear of failure, which was listed by 30% of Turkish respondents as a reason why they would give up on any entrepreneurial pursuits (Karadeniz, 2011).

Economic development promotes quality jobs for local people

During the OECD study visit, the development agency and municipality officials were asked whether they actively market the local labour force to potential inward investors; they declared that general information (without reference to human capital) is provided to potential investors but some information on local skills and human capital would only be made available upon request. It should be noted, however, that this information would not be based on locally collected data and systematic analyses of local labour markets. Typically, the information shared is made up of data collected by Turkstat on a given labour market, attendance to training courses opened by local İŞKUR and student enrolment at local vocational schools, coupled with personal observations from local officials. No significant sign of a culture of actively marketing local areas has been observed among the local officials interviewed, this being particularly true for officials appointed by the central government.

Municipality officials stated that it is standard practice to consider the potential number of jobs to be created for local residents when taking decisions concerning inward investment. There may also be some *ad hoc* consideration about the quality of jobs to be created by such investments, but there appears to be no strategic planning that takes into account any multiplier effects. The number of jobs to be created immediately by a company undertaking green field investment in a given province is often considered in isolation from the job creation process that this initial investment will trigger over the medium to long-run. Any consideration of the multiplier effects of the initial investment on the future quality of local jobs is even scanter. Development Agency and municipality officials interviewed for this OECD study said that there were no actions to ensure that bids for local development and construction projects include job and training opportunities to local residents.

Being inclusive

Figure 3.10. **OECD Dashboard results for being inclusive**

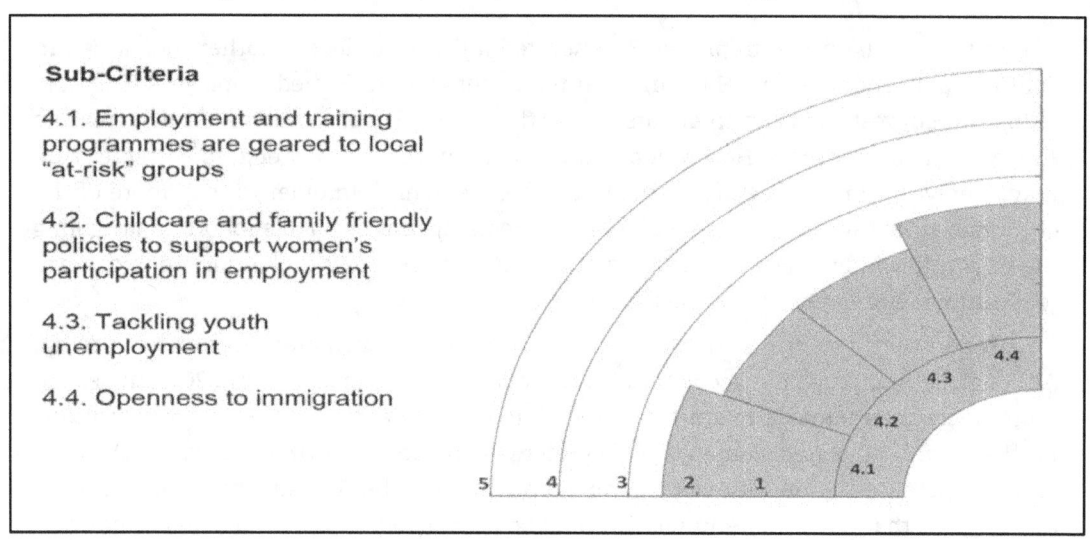

Employment and training programmes geared to local "at risk" groups

At 43%, Turkey has the highest gender participation gap among OECD countries. This gap is one of the highest even among emerging economies, although it has narrowed somewhat over recent years (OECD 2016b). Women also face much poorer job quality than men in Turkey. In 2015, 46.1% of female workers had informal jobs compared with 28.2% for men (Turkstat, 2015). Women also earn on average almost 21% less than men, which represented a gender pay gap that is above average by OECD standards (OECD, 2015).

Special programmes are delivered for various groups identified to be at-risk but data in this policy area is scarce. The Social Security Institution (SGK) has a nationwide hot line for unregistered workers to file complaints against their employers or seek legal assistance, with SGK offices also providing the same services. There are legal provisions requiring companies of a certain size to hire workers with disabilities and ex-convicts.

Local İŞKUR offices and municipalities try to help with the matching process but employers are often unwilling to fill these quotas. In Kocaeli, the Municipality itself hires some convicts on parole. There are also programmes developed for people on rehabilitation for drug or alcohol abuse. A few training programmes are delivered through outreach directly into disadvantaged communities such as the Romanis or the Roma.

Kocaeli Municipality played an active role in an innovative project whereby a foundation (*Bizim Köy Engelliler Vakfı*) has been established to facilitate employment of people with various disabilities. The foundation brings together civil society organisations under the patronage of the local Chamber of Industry and provides incentives to a number of local firms that specifically hire workers with disabilities. Kocaeli Municipality also takes on interns with disabilities via an internship programme for local students. Southern Marmara Development Agency (MARKA), which covers Kocaeli, declared the "increasing participation of 'disadvantaged groups' in social and economic life" as the number one priority area of support in its Social Development Grants Programme for 2013.

Specific training programmes are provided to local at-risk groups, with assistance being offered to trainees. Kocaeli Municipality, for example, offers vocational training courses (KOMEK) and provides child care services to the children of participants free of charge. During the OECD study visit, the Deputy Secretary General noted that the Municipality would be more than willing to provide free transport to people taking UMEM courses or similar vocational training through the public system.

The UMEM project is noteworthy as this project allows people who register themselves as unemployed in İŞKUR's database while working informally (e.g. without a SGK registration) to enrol in an UMEM course which will enable them to find new formal jobs at the end of their training.

Box 3.5. **Best Practice Example: "Our Village" Project in Kocaeli**

Initiated in 2005 as a European Union-funded project led by the Kocaeli Chamber of Industry for the Engagement of Disadvantaged Groups, 'Our Village Productivity Centre' is a production area comprised of manufacturing and agricultural facilities in which 85% of people employed have various disabilities.

Inspiration for the project came from the difficulties that many local employers faced in filling legal quotas for employing disabled workers. Employers either find it difficult to create suitable positions for people with disabilities along the production line or to identify disabled people with the required skills to fill certain jobs. Fulfilling the legal requirements by filling disabled worker quotas proved to be a common problem faced by employers all over the country. In many instances, employers hire disabled people whose skills do not match their needs in order to meet to the disabled worker quotas.

The project was initiated as a joint effort that brought together public and private stakeholders, including civil society foundations. With the capacity to employ a total of 230 people, the centre employed 92 people as of December 2015, 79 of whom were disabled. The wages and salaries of current employees are paid by different companies that jointly "own" the centre and each disabled employee whose salary is paid by a certain company or employer is counted towards the fulfilment of the legal quota for that company or employer.

As such, the project is linking employment to social inclusion efforts. The project is noteworthy not only for enabling people with disabilities to get integrated into local labour markets but also for establishing an exemplary public-private partnership to boost local employment opportunities.

Childcare and other policies to support women's participation in labour force

Most families in both provinces can access subsidised childcare outside the home but the supply of these services falls short of demand. This may hinder the career of many working mothers whose only option is to hire baby sitters, which may not be affordable or reliable. Some schemes are in place to increase participation in early years' education amongst disadvantaged groups, such as the children of immigrants, but it is doubtful that these schemes reach all disadvantaged groups. Education in early years is a priority area in Kocaeli's public investment plans. In addition, the Governor's Office provides financial support to poor families that have difficulty in covering child care expenses.

There are relatively few initiatives concerning the care for the elderly outside the home. However, a relatively recent nationwide initiative introduced by the government allows housewives taking care of an elderly family member *at home* to get paid in return for the home-based care they provide. This initiative aims to financially support families that have to provide home-based care for the elderly member, rather than facilitate participation in the labour force. Locally, no systematic step has been taken to work with employers to implement family friendly policies. There is an innovative pilot study that is currently being conducted in three provinces – Antalya, Bursa and Izmir – which is intended to measure the effectiveness of child care subsidies on the labour force participation of women (see Box 3.6). If the pilot study produces promising results, the subsidies may become a nationwide policy.

Box 3.6. Nanny subsidies for working mothers

There is a project funded by the Ministry of Labour and Social Security and co-financed by the European Union entitled "Supporting Formal Employment of Women through Child Care Services at Home". Aimed at ensuring and sustaining formal employment of women, the project got started as a pilot study undertaken with the participation of 5 000 mothers and 5 000 care-givers in three provinces: Antalya, Bursa and Izmir. Mothers who work full time on a service contract or who seek employment for the first time employ registered caregivers (or register their current caregivers who are employed informally) benefit from state subsidies amounting to 300 Euros a month on the average (maximum subsidy of 390 Euros is provided to single mothers; to the mothers of children with disabilities, or to mothers who choose to employ a care-giver with a national qualification certificate or a Ministry of Education/İŞKUR-trained and certified care giver) for a period of 24 months.

The main objective of the project are to

- Increase the labour participation rate of women and the share of registered (as opposed to informal) female workers (according to 2014 statistics, 46% of all working women are in informal employment);
- Facilitate the return of mothers to work as quickly as possible after delivering their babies, as well as enabling mothers with young children to enter the labour force;
- Support the formal employment of women who work in domestic services (currently about 92% of women employed as domestic workers work informally);
- Improve the quality of child care given at home;
- Ensure that children receive quality care.

Eligible mothers must have Turkish citizenship; be residing (with their child/children) in one of the provinces covered in the pilot study; have completed their maternity leave; have a child (0-24 months) at the time of pre-registration; have pre-tax earnings of no more than

> **Box 3.6. Nanny subsidies for working mothers** (cont.)
>
> twice the gross amount of monthly minimum wage; not be making a living as caregiver herself throughout the duration of the project.
>
> Eligible caregivers must have Turkish citizenship; be residing in one of the provinces covered in the pilot study; not be a first degree relative of either parent of the child(ren) – up to the third degree if the caregiver lives with the parents; be a registered worker paying social security contributions (registration must be completed by the first day of work at the latest); be 18 years or older and have at least a primary school degree.
>
> The programme features an audit phase. For example, mothers need to make the monthly payments (including premiums) to the caregivers in full. The Project team carry out home visits in order to check if the conditions for the payment of the subsidy are fulfilled. The subsidy is cut in cases where the caregivers turn out to be absent without excuse during three home visits or if the due payments to caregivers are not made on time for three times. For one child, the maximum duration of receipt is 24 months (when the child has completed 36 months of age). There is a grace period of one month for violation of some of the eligibility conditions due to unforeseen circumstances like mothers losing their jobs; caregivers quitting or getting sacked throughout the period of subsidy. Mothers are given a month to find a new job or caregiver under such circumstances. In case a mother losing her jobs seeks employment through İŞKUR and continues employing caregivers, she will continue receiving subsidies.
>
> Source: SGK and ÇSGB, "Evde Çocuk Bakımı-Bilgilendirme Broşürü" (2015).

Tackling youth unemployment

The 2016 OECD Employment Outlook highlights how vulnerable youth are of particular concern in Turkey, which has one of the highest youth unemployment rates among OECD countries (OECD, 2016). Nearly 30% of young people in Turkey aged 15-29 are NEET (i.e. not in education, employment or training). This figure is sharply lower than in 2007 but well

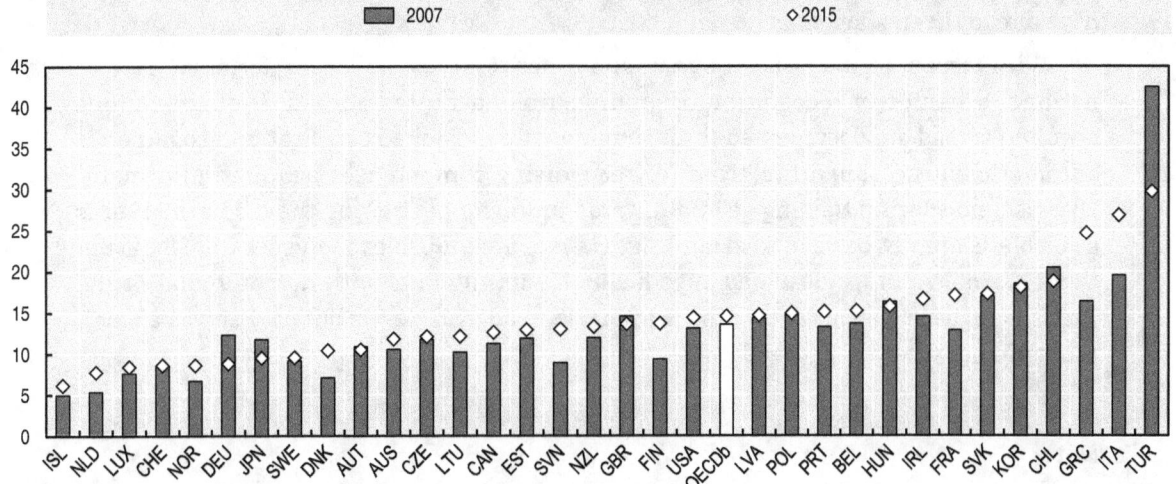

Figure 3.11. **Percentage of youth aged 15-29 who are neither employed nor in education or training, 2007 and 2015**

a) The NEET rate has been estimated and may include unemployed persons who are studying.
b) Selected urban areas only.
Source: OECD (2016a), http://dx.doi.org/10.1787/empl_outlook-2016-graph14-en.

above the OECD average of nearly 15%. Low skills are a key barrier to achieving better labour market outcomes for youth in Turkey: nearly one in five young people in Turkey are low-skilled NEETs – compared to around one in 20 in OECD countries.

Looking at the case study areas, some *ad hoc* initiatives exist to support students who drop out of school, either bringing them back into education or aiding their transition into the labour market. But these initiatives are not systematic. The İŞKUR director of Kocaeli, for example, said that they would look into the possibilities for collaboration when there is a project proposal to address the issue. A notable initiative has been introduced in Kocaeli through the "White Hearts" (*Beyaz Kalpler*) project. The programme aims to identify young people who are likely to drop out of school and to convince them to stay in school or get their education through alternative channels. It should be noted that no analysis to assess the number of NEETS has been carried out in either case study area.

Openness to immigration

Turkey has recently become a net recipient of migrants from neighbouring countries, particularly from the Caucasus and the Balkans as well as countries as far as Afghanistan and Pakistan, and sub-Saharan African nations. Many of the migrants come in the search for jobs. Others, particularly the Afghans and Pakistanis, flee wars and poor living conditions in their countries and see Turkey largely as a transit country for temporary stay in their way towards Europe.

The country has also experienced a very large influx of Syrian refugees fleeing the civil war that started in 2011. As of March 2016, the estimated number of Syrians in Turkey has reached 3 million. There has been considerable progress in registering some of the migrants with special ID numbers and issuing work permits, particularly for migrants from neighbouring countries working as care givers and baby sitters. However, only limited steps have been taken to integrate the huge population of Syrian and other refugees into society and labour markets as legal and registered, albeit temporary, workers. It was initially thought that Syrian refugees would only be welcomed in refugee camps for a reasonably short period of time before returning to their country, which may explain why no comprehensive action has been taken to integrate these refugees into society or the labour markets. Policies and actions are currently being planned and some preliminary legal texts have already been adopted.

With respect to the skills of Syrian and other refugees, no local referral is made to national schemes in recognition of qualifications acquired abroad. If qualifications acquired abroad are documented through nationally accredited certificates, recognition is automatic but no support is given for recognising competences acquired informally. Likewise, no specific training geared towards immigrants entering the labour market is available. Currently, basic Turkish language courses are available to refugees from Syria but there are no trainings designed specifically for immigrants with no command of the Turkish language. Language training is available to all skills levels but only serves a small proportion of potential demand.

Note

1. *Provincial Boards of Vocational Education* (PVEBs) that previously served as local platforms for stakeholder communication to improve the VET system and to strengthen its ties to local labour markets were converted into *Provincial Boards of Employment and Vocational Education* (PEVTBs) in 2008. PEVTBs

enabled the provincial network of İŞKUR to get integrated into the local PVEBs thereby creating a larger platform to identify local courses of action in finding the balance between demands of employers and capabilities of the central government in each province.

References

Bizimköy Engelliler Üretim Merkezi, official webpage available at www.bizimkoy.org.tr/.

DOKA (2014), *Doğu Karadeniz Bölgesinde Arap Turizmi-Mevcut Durum ve Gelişme Stratejisi Raporu*, Trabzon: DOKA.

ETF (2015), *Torino Process 2014 Turkey*, Torino: European Training Foundation.

EU Commission Turkey Delegation, *Bizimköy Engelliler Üretim Merkezi* webpage available at http://avrupa.info.tr/tr/bilgi-kaynaklari/haber-arsivi/news-single-view/article/avrupa-komisyonu-tuerkiye-delegasyonu-bizimkoey-engelliler-ueretim-merkezine-proje.html.

Giguère, S. and F. Froy (2009), "A New Framework for Labour Market Policy in a Global Economy", in Flexible Policy for More and Better Jobs, OECD Publishing, http://dx.doi.org/10.1787/9789264059528-3-en.

İŞKUR (2016a), "Career and Job Counselling Services", www.iskur.gov.tr/tr-tr/kurumsalbilgi/istatistikler.aspx#dltop.

İŞKUR (2016b), "Counsellor visits to workplaces", www.iskur.gov.tr/tr-tr/kurumsalbilgi/istatistikler.aspx#dltop.

İŞKUR (2014a), *Kocaeli 2014 İşgücü Piyasası Araştırma Raporu*, Kocaeli Çalışma ve İş Kurumu İl Müdürlüğü.

İŞKUR (2014b), *Trabzon 2014 İşgücü Piyasası Araştırma Raporu*, Trabzon Çalışma ve İş Kurumu İl Müdürlüğü.

Karadeniz, E. (2011), *Entrepreneurship in Turkey 2010*, Global Entrepreneurship Monitor.

Kocaeli-Doğu Marmara İstihdam Fuarı available at www.domif.org/.

Kocaeli Sanayi Odası, *Bizimköy Engelliler Üretim Merkezi* webpage available at www.kosano.org.tr/bizimkoy-engelliler-uretim-merkezi.

Milliyet, *Bizimköy Engelliler Üretim Merkezi*, www.milliyet.com.tr/Local/Article?ID=1095460, accessed 3 December, 2015.

OECD (2017), "Job quality", OECD Employment and Labour Market Statistics (database), http://dx.doi.org/10.1787/e357cdbf-en.

OECD (2016a), *OECD Employment Outlook 2016*, OECD Publishing, Paris, http://dx.doi.org/10.1787/empl_outlook-2016-en.

OECD (2016b), "Regional labour markets", OECD Regional Statistics (database), http://dx.doi.org/10.1787/f7445d96-en.

OECD (2016c), *Self-employment rate (indicator)*, http://dx.doi.org/10.1787/fb58715e-en.

OECD (2015), "Turkey", in *Education at a Glance 2015: OECD Indicators*, OECD Publishing, Paris, http://dx.doi.org/10.1787/eag-2015-84-en.

OECD (2014), *OECD Employment Outlook 2014*, OECD Publishing, Paris, http://dx.doi.org/10.1787/empl_outlook-2014-en.

OECD (2013), "Turkey", in *Education at a Glance 2013: OECD Indicators*, OECD Publishing, Paris, http://dx.doi.org/10.1787/eag-2013-75-en.

Trabzon İstihdam Fuarı available at http://trabzonikage.org.

Turkstat (2015), Data available at https://biruni.tuik.gov.tr/medas/?kn=116&locale=en and Interactive Statistics available at www.tuik.gov.tr/PreTablo.do?alt_id=1046.

World Bank (2014), *Turkey Workforce Development*, SABER (Systems Assessment for Better Education Results) Country Report 2012.

Yüksek Öğretim Kurumu-YÖK, Higher Education Council Statistics available at https://istatistik.yok.gov.tr/.

Chapter 4

Towards an action plan for jobs in Turkey: Recommendations and best practices

> Stimulating job creation at the local level requires integrated actions across employment, training and economic development portfolios. This requires policies which can be catered to the local level, up-to-date and accurate data, and integrated partnerships that leverage the efforts of stakeholders. This chapter outlines the key recommendations emerging from the review of local job creation policies in Turkey, looking at local employment and economic development strategies in Kocaeli and Trabzon.

Towards an action plan for jobs: Recommendations for Turkey

Overall recommendations
Better aligning programmes and policies to local economic development • Establish local strategic planning processes to integrate employment and economic development efforts. • Develop stronger local research and analytical capacities by leveraging the role of universities in producing labour market information and forecasting skills needs. **Adding value through skills** • Encourage more partnerships between the training system and employers to ensure that skills development programmes are well connected to labour market demand. **Targeting policy to local employment sectors and investing in quality jobs** • Foster the better use of talent in the workplace to boost quality job creation and the productive capacities of local economies. **Being inclusive** • Launch a youth employment strategy at the national level and identify innovative local approaches, which could be adapted to other regions in Turkey. • Urgently re-focus labour market integration efforts to assist migrants in developing employability skills.

Recommendations for the case study areas	
Trabzon • Launch skills development programmes focused on the tourism sector to improve the services available and promote the sector's job creation potential. • Build stronger partnerships with the university sector to reduce skills mismatches and align curriculum to the local labour market • Establish pilot programmes, which encourage employers to think more strategically about their workforce and human resources management to promote job quality.	**Kocaeli** • Develop pilot programmes, which help local manufacturers improve their use of technology and better connect them to global value chains. • Increase the number of youth and employers participating in apprenticeship and other work-based training programmes. • Work with large employers to raise awareness on the importance of human resource management issues and encourage them to use their supply chain management practices to assist small and medium-sized enterprises (SMEs) to undertake more skills training.

Better aligning policies and programmes towards local economic development

Recommendation: Establish local strategic planning processes to integrate employment and economic development efforts.

At the regional and local level, Provincial Boards of Employment and Vocational Education (PEVTBs) provide a formal governance platform to bring together a broad range of employment, skills and economic development actors to discuss labour market issues. These boards are expected to identify unique local challenges and potential programme solutions to address them. When a consensus is reached by the board, they issue mandatory decisions on which employment and skills policies should be taken at the local level.

However, local employment and economic planning is often based on short-term considerations, which reflects the duration of appointments for İŞKUR and Ministry of National Education senior officials, which typically last no longer than 4-5 years. These officials also tend to be non-locals assigned to posts for a limited period of time. This means that most public officials are unlikely to spend a long duration of their career in the province where they are currently assigned, which limits the sense of community ownership among public officials. There is also a strong culture of central administration in Turkey, which can impact on the willingness of local stakeholders to formulate innovative policy solutions for the local labour market.

Going forward, the government should consider establishing a more formal strategic planning process, which integrates employment and economic development objectives. Local development plans in Trabzon and Kocaeli (and other provinces in Turkey) should be formulated on a more systematic basis, which defines local employment and economic development opportunities as well as the necessary actions that need to be taken to achieve the region's potential. This strategic planning process should involve local actors working together to articulate a vision for the local economy and the priority sectors that need to be developed for future job creation and growth. Currently, it appears that this type of long-term integrated planning process does not exist at the local level.

For example, in both Trabzon and Kocaeli, priority sectors for local development have been articulated through provincial development board meetings and similar forums attended by local stakeholders, or through informal vision development or foresight exercises undertaken by specific local actors, such as the Chamber of Industry. However, there is no indication as to the existence of well-defined action plans that formally assign roles to each local stakeholder to ensure effective follow-up action is taken and then evaluated. In the development of such plans, there is an opportunity for regional development agencies to play a greater role in identifying and co-ordinating possible actions with the broader range of employment and skills stakeholders. İŞKUR would also need to play an active role in any long-term strategic planning process to ensure that employment and training opportunities can be created around the priority sectors identified and better anticipate skills needs in the future.

Currently, there is little evidence that the compatibility of the supply of skills within the *existing* labour force is given serious consideration in the identification of strategic growth sectors. For example, the local economic development visions in Kocaeli and Trabzon seemed to involve expansion to higher tech/higher value-added industries, even though such developments may not align with the existing supply of skills. A revised strategic planning process in Turkey should ensure that provinces conduct a skills gap analysis, which takes into account their existing stock of skills and how it can effectively contribute to job creation in the future. Turkey could look to the Local Workforce Investment Boards in the United States (see Box 4.1), which are required to undertake a strategic planning process as part of their management of the employment and skills system.

Going forward in Turkey, a small task force in each province could be established to focus on local employment and economic development opportunities over the long-term. Ideally, this type of task force should comprise experts/representatives from the regional development agency, the local universities and local chambers and the provincial directorate of İŞKUR. They should study possible employment scenarios and the associated skill needs of various local development strategies (e.g. whether it makes sense to promote the expansion of different types of industries or expand into new economic areas) and report their findings at least twice a year at the relevant Provincial Employment and Vocational Training Board (PEVTB). The reports of these task forces should explicitly state any trade-offs and bottlenecks associated with each local development scenario, to allow for systematic and constructive policy debate based on evidence and analysis at the PEVTB and other forums.

Given the limited local capacities in many provinces, however, these task forces should be led by a team leader to be chosen from a pool of well-trained staff at the İŞKUR headquarters in Ankara, and assigned to a unit responsible for that province at the General Directorate. Ideally, the İŞKUR's headquarters should have a template to evaluate future

> **Box 4.1. OECD example: Strategic planning by Local Workforce Investment Boards in the United States**
>
> Under the Workforce Innovation and Opportunity Act, nearly 600 Local Workforce Investment Areas (LWIAs) and close to 3 000 One-Stop Career Centres have been established. The local Workforce Investment Boards (WIBs) administer WIOA services as designated by the Governor of their state and within the regulations of the federal statute and US Department of Labor (USDOL) guidelines. Members of local workforce investment boards are appointed by local elected officials in accordance with criteria established by the Governor. Local WIBs are typically an extension of a local government unit, which in most cases is the county government and can include more than one government entity. Local WIBs are not agencies of the federal or state governments, and their staff is not comprised of federal or state employees.
>
> Local WIBs are governed by a board comprised of business and civic leaders and, to a lesser extent, representatives of social service organisations, educational agencies and labour groups. WIA requires at least 51% of the board members to be business leaders so that the needs of businesses are readily taken into account in designing and delivering employment services.
>
> The local WIB develops and submits a local area plan to the Governor, appoints local one-stop operators, and selects eligible organisations to provide services for youth and adults. Local and state Workforce Investment Boards are held accountable through common measures of performance for each of the three WIA programmes. For the two adult programmes, the common measures are based on employment outcomes – the ability of the programme participant to find and retain a decent-paying job upon leaving the programme.
>
> WIOA requires that the Governor of each state submit a WIA/Wagner-Peyser State Plan to USDOL that outlines a five-year strategy for its workforce investment system. USDOL must approve the state plan in order for the state to receive formula allotments under WIA or financial assistance under Wagner-Peyser. Each local WIB is also required to develop and submit a plan for the Governor's approval. The content of the plan is very similar to the state plan. As in the state plan, the local plan must include an analysis of the workforce investment needs of businesses, job seekers and workers in the area, the current and projected employment opportunities in the local area, and the job skills necessary to obtain such employment opportunities. The local plan must also include a description of the activities it intends to pursue to meet the identified needs; the memoranda of understanding it has established between itself and each of its one-stop partners; and performance targets negotiated between the local board and the Governor.
>
> Source: OECD (2014a), *Employment and Skills Strategies in the United States*, OECD Reviews on Local Job Creation, OECD Publishing, Paris, http://dx.doi.org/10.1787/9789264209398-en.

local employment and economic development strategies in each province. This should be prepared in such a way to provide a general framework of evaluation, recognising the uniqueness and aspirations of each provincial economy, while also keeping in mind the need for innovative local inputs. The team leader from the provincial unit could attend a pre-determined number of task force meetings in the province, to effectively lead the group. Likewise, İŞKUR could bring together task force members across Turkey annually for a progress evaluation meeting where local experiences could be shared and policy ideas could be exchanged.

Recommendation: Develop stronger local research and analytical capacities by leveraging the role of universities in producing labour market information and forecasting skills needs.

There is an opportunity to make better use of capacities available at local universities to develop labour market evaluations and forecasting reports, which look at the skill needs of the local economy. While some collaborative initiatives involving local universities do exist, it appears that there is room to strengthen these types of collaborations in both Trabzon and Kocaeli. For example, Kocaeli University has recently led a study looking at the job creation potential of the Information and Community Technology (ICT) sector for the province. These types of studies should be emulated by other universities in Turkey and could also serve as a useful input into any longer-term strategic planning process.

Under such a scenario, local universities would become more engaged in the production of labour market information, which offer insights into the competitive position of Turkish provinces and sector specific analysis, which could compare the strengths and weaknesses of the local economy. This type of analysis would provide local stakeholders with a more comprehensive understanding of the labour market and point to specific policy areas where action is needed. Labour market information is often the "glue" which can further sustain and strengthen local partnerships. It can also help local stakeholders to develop a shared understanding of potential challenges. Lastly, information can serve as a "call to action", which can propel public actors into taking concrete steps to improve the competitive position of their province. İŞKUR could play a role in this type of exercise by launching a call for proposals across Turkey to local academics to produce provincially specific labour market studies, which build awareness and knowledge around employment and economic development issues at the regional level in Turkey.

Adding value through skills

Recommendation: Establish stronger linkages between the training system and local employers to ensure that skills development programmes are well connected to labour market demand.

In Turkey, there are major challenges concerning to school to work transitions. Several concrete measures such as the addition of career guidance topics and several key competencies to the curricula at schools have been taken since 2010. To facilitate this transition, however, gaps between skills acquired at schools and skills needed in the labour market need to be addressed more effectively. In general, the government needs to expand access to apprenticeships, work-place training programmes as well as opportunities for modular learning. Stronger mechanisms, which encourage and expand communication between employers and policy makers, and improvements to the consultation interface that allows dissemination of knowledge across all stakeholders in the vocational education and training (VET) system would also enable smoother school to work transitions, while helping to address potential skills mismatches at the local level. The experience with provincial Course Management Boards of the UMEM project is valuable in this context and provides a useful basis to design mechanisms to increase employer involvement.

During the OECD study visit, many local stakeholders in Kocaeli and Trabzon noted the importance of involving employers more in the design and development of employment and training programmes. Employers have a key role to play in defining their labour market needs and working with the vocational education and training system to ensure that skills are being developed to align with local labour market demand. Currently, it appears that employer engagement could be strengthened in Turkey through stronger communication and co-ordinated outreach among public actors at the local level. In particular, employers could play a stronger advisory role with the vocational education and training system, advising on course content and service delivery arrangements. Box 4.2 provides an international example from Ontario, Canada, where employers play a direct role in advising local community colleges on course content and curriculum.

> **Box 4.2. OECD example: Programme Advisory Committees in Ontario, Canada**
>
> In Ontario, Canada, each community college (i.e. VET institution) has a Programme Advisory Committee (PAC), which is composed of employers, to assist in keeping the programmes offerings relevant and to alert the colleges to training gaps. Programme Advisory Committees report to the President of the college through a Board of Governors. PACs help to define graduate requirements and course content.
>
> Source: OECD (2014b), *Employment and Skills Strategies in Canada*, OECD Reviews on Local Job Creation, OECD Publishing, Paris.

Several local stakeholders noted that some smaller provinces knowingly offer vocational training programmes, which encourage the unemployed to acquire skills demanded by businesses located in other provinces rather than the local industry, effectively acting as skill "exporters" within Turkey. While this could be a meaningful local economic development strategy, to the extent that such emigration will later generate remittances receipts or investments – particularly if other constraints (such as the small size of the local market) prevent further development of local industry, it is ultimately sub-optimal for the training sector to be offering these types of courses.

In particular, apprenticeships are a key skills development mechanism, which enable learners to develop a good mix of generic and occupationally specific skills. Beyond the apprenticeship system, there is scope in Turkey to increase the scope and intensity of other types of work-based training opportunities which lead to good career progression opportunities and pathways within a workplace or sector. The role of employer associations is particularly important, as they can act as a means to improve SME engagement and function as a buffer to make sure training is not too tailored to the demands of a single industry. Box 4.3 provides an international example from the UK, where local apprenticeship hubs have been established to coordinate outreach with employers (especially SMEs) and encourage their participation in apprenticeship programmes.

> **Box 4.3. OECD example: Local apprenticeship hubs in the United Kingdom**
>
> There has also been a recent push to increase the number of apprenticeships in the UK at both the upper-secondary and post-secondary levels. Apprenticeships have received significant policy attention under the last two UK governments, with the number in England doubling since 2010. The recent establishment of new local institutional structures (e.g. Combined Authorities) and the devolution of funding and greater responsibility to local areas to support economic growth (e.g. via City Deals/Local Growth Deals) is providing new opportunities for UK cities to lead, shape and implement skills strategies.
>
> As part of the City Deal process, the city Manchester and Leeds have decided to invest in skills, with a priority focus on apprenticeships. In Manchester a new Apprenticeship and Skills Hub was set up in 2012-13 with a budget of six million pounds to increase the number

> **Box 4.3. OECD example: Local apprenticeship hubs in the United Kingdom**
> *(cont.)*
>
> of people taking apprenticeships at level 3 and above, and to support apprenticeships within SMEs. The initial aim was to increase the number of 16-24 year olds starting apprenticeships by 10% a year every year until 2017/18, however this target was later abandoned.
>
> A primary aim of the Apprenticeships Hub was to maximise demand for apprenticeships from employers, by carrying out marketing exercises, encouraging the public sector to provide civic leadership by taking on apprentices, and building capacities amongst smaller employers to recruit and manage apprentices. At the same time, there has been a campaign to increase the take up of apprenticeships amongst young people through the investment in careers advice and guidance in schools. A third aim has been to boost the capacity of local training providers to develop higher-level apprenticeships in growth sectors within the Manchester economy. To date most of the work of the Apprenticeship Hub has focused on the following:
>
> i) **Providing information, advice and guidance to young people:** The emphasis given in Greater Manchester to the promotion of information, advice and guidance for young people has reflected broader concerns about careers advice in schools and colleges, and the extent to which vocational training and apprenticeships were being promoted.
>
> ii) **Building capacity amongst training providers:** The second main area of activity in Greater Manchester to date has been building capacity in the training provider sector, particularly in the field of higher and advanced level apprenticeships.
>
> iii) **Engaging employers:** A key priority for Greater Manchester has been to engage more small to medium size enterprises or SMEs, of which there are 97 000 in Greater Manchester. The learning so far is that this process is partly about managing the expectations amongst these employers as to what makes somebody 'job ready' at the age of 19.
>
> The Greater Manchester apprenticeships hub is overseen by a core partnership involving the ten Greater Manchester Local Authorities, the Chamber of Commerce, the Skills Funding Agency, the Learning Provider Network, the Colleges Group and the North West Business Leadership team. These organisations are involved in project commissioning and steering. The core partners meet every four months and there are sub-groups, for example focusing on marketing (the latter involves a business representative and a young apprentice).
>
> Source: OECD (2017a, forthcoming), *Engaging employers in apprenticeship opportunities at the local level*, OECD Publishing, Paris.

Investing in quality jobs and stimulating productivity

Recommendation: Foster the better utilisation of skills to boost quality job creation and the productive capacities of local economies.

Creating quality jobs is a key pillar towards an effective employment and skill system. This means considering how skills are developed but also how they are put to use by employers. When employers are demanding a higher level of skills as a result of the employment opportunities available, it will result in greater skills development opportunities as well as innovation within the training system. Previous OECD research has highlighted that resources in Turkey do not flow enough from lower to higher-productivity activities, despite ever greater government incentives to promote formal businesses investment in selected regions and sectors (OECD, 2014d).

İŞKUR should re-examine its suite of employment and training programmes to ensure a focus on higher productivity activities that stimulate the demand for skills through incentives, which encourage stronger entrepreneurship and skills development opportunities within SMEs. This would involve looking at how to move low value-added sectors into higher value-added production through technology transfer and adoption. Local universities and the VET sector can play an important role in this regard by working locally with employers to conduct applied research as well as sharing knowledge on the use of technology in the production process. Box 4.4 provides an international example from Korea, which has seen success in this policy area.

> ### Box 4.4. **OECD example: KOREATECH Bridge Model**
>
> The KOREATECH Bridge Model fosters training together among large and small-medium size firms. The local university (KOREATECH) plays a role in bridging the technology gap between large and smaller employers. The KOREATECH bridge model comprises a three-way academia-industry partnership involving a major enterprise, its partner SMEs and KOREATECH. The university offers an Employment Training Programme which offers short-term courses to employees of participating firms.
>
> This bridge model was first pioneered by Samsung Electronics and its sub-contractors in 2006. Samsung and KOREATECH collaborated to build an Advanced Technology Education Centre and jointly conducted demand surveys to develop relevant programme curriculum. Samsung contributed technical knowledge, equipment, and industry experts to co-teach courses. Samsung's sub-contractors contributed employee to be trained in Samsung's latest technology and KOREATECH provides the facilities and operates the centre. The Bridge Model's success has led to its expanded application across 11 universities in Korea by 45 medium enterprise and 2 268 SMEs.
>
> KOREATECH has also established the Leaders Industry-University Co-operation (LINK Project) which fosters working professional in specific sectors. The project is designed to expand and advance entrepreneurship within the education system as well as to foster strong industry-university linkages.
>
> Source: OECD (2014c), *Employment and Skills Strategies in Korea*, OECD Publishing, Paris, http://dx.doi.org/10.1787/9789264216563-en.

In general, stronger co-ordination is needed (both horizontally among local actors and vertically between local and national agencies) regarding how to effectively reach out to employers to stimulate innovation and productivity through the best use of skills and effective work organisation programmes. İŞKUR could play a stronger role in sharing success stories of training programmes within SMEs, which have stimulated innovation and productivity.

At the local level, job and vocational counsellors within İŞKUR provide an effective mechanism to ensure that employment services are working with employers to identify job opportunities and match unemployed people to jobs. These counsellors are well connected to the local labour market and have established valuable connections with a number of employers. They could be given a "steer" to work with employers on skills utilisation and work organisation issues. In some cases, employers may not be able to find appropriate candidates because the job on offer is of poor quality therefore it is important to work with employers to stimulate a stronger demand for skills in the labour market. Box 4.5 provides

> **Box 4.5. OECD example: Public employment services in Quebec, Canada working with employers on human resources practices**
>
> In recent years, Emploi-Québec has been focusing on working with employers on human resource management practices under the assumption that employers who employ good human resource practices tend to have better operations with more stable and productive employees. The resources available, however, limit the number of employers that can be visited. Two specialised centres in the Montreal regional office of Emploi-Québec are intended to support and encourage better use of skills on the part of employers including on the following issues:
>
> - Diagnosis of human resource issues;
> - Support management (coaching);
> - The establishment of a consultative committee within the company so that it can adapt to major changes that could jeopardise jobs; this committee analyses the difficulties, proposes solutions and sees to the implementation of an action plan and its monitoring.
> - The human resource management support by a specialist to notably improve ways to make recruitment, skills development, retention or Performance Evaluation
> - The establishment of a human resources department.
>
> Sector labour committees supported by the Labour Market Partners Commission are taking a greater interest in developing workplace capabilities and are offering work analysis to facilitate job laddering within the sector. This can help employers look at internal development of employees as an option to external recruitment as well as better assist employees in making career decisions, including investments in continuing education.
>
> Businesses could make greater use of this solution, given existing recruiting problems in certain areas and the fact that workforce ageing could exacerbate the difficulties in the future. An increasing role of the committees is to promote improvements in the organisation of work and better use of labour. Activities include sharing of best practices, thematic comparisons and pooled development of training.
>
> *Source:* OECD (2016b), "Montréal : Métropole de talent – Pistes d'action pour améliorer l'emploi, l'innovation et les compétences", *OECD LEED Working Paper*, available at www.oecd.org/fr/emploi/leed/montreal-metropole-talent-2016.htm.

an example from Quebec, Canada, where the local public employment service is directing involved in working with employers on human resources and organisational management practices to improve job quality.

Being inclusive

Recommendation: Launch a youth employment strategy at the national level and identify innovative local approaches, which could be adapted in other regions of Turkey.

This report has highlighted the significant labour market challenges faced by youth in Turkey. Among OECD countries, Turkey has the highest youth unemployment rate; in addition, there is a significant number of youth who are NEETs (i.e. not in education, employment of training). Many youth in Turkey are low-skilled individuals, which impacts their probability of labour market success.

The government should launch a youth employment strategy, which would aim to reduce the overall unemployment rate among youth while also ensuring that they are given greater access to education and skills development opportunities. In particular, it is important to better link youth to apprenticeships, internships and other work-based learning opportunities, which will enable them to develop a balanced mix of generic and occupational-specific skills. As part of this process, it would be important to engage local employers to understand the potential disconnect between their hiring expectations and the aspirations of youth. Long periods of unemployment for youth have been shown to have potential "scarring" effects, which have a harmful impact in later life, particularly for NEET youth. It can lower future income levels, skills validity, future employability, job satisfaction, happiness and health levels.

Ensuring employment success for young people is a policy issue of particular relevance locally. Barriers preventing young people from successful transition into employment are often multifaceted in nature and responses need to come from a wide array of policy areas. It is at the local level that government policies can be integrated and combined with place-based initiatives to provide multidimensional responses to complex problems. Yet, in practice, programmes are too often delivered in isolation from each other, with uneven degrees of coverage and limited capacity to reach out to the most in need. Rigid policy delivery frameworks, insufficient capacities and a lack of strategic approach at the local level are often the reasons that undermine support for youth.

Turkey can look at approaches that have been taken in other OECD countries at the local level. Reliable data is a prerequisite for effective policy design. However, many localities in Turkey are confronted with serious challenges when compiling data to diagnose the nature of youth unemployment locally.

Box 4.6 provides an international example of a youth employment strategy that was introduced in Glasgow, Scotland. It demonstrates the importance of designing a performance management system that better connects stakeholders at the local level. In Brandenburg, Germany, there is continuous monitoring of the supply and demand of skills, as a result of discussions with local companies and schools. This monitoring informs local strategies and action plans, which are developed on the ground between the different relevant actors. The monitoring also includes forecasting of the supply of students graduating from schools over the next 10-15 years.

> ### Box 4.6. **Youth unemployment: Tackling fragmentation in Glasgow, United Kingdom**
>
> The city of Glasgow has re-engineered its approach to supporting youth employability since the mid-2000s; and since the recession hit, NEET figures have not risen dramatically compared to Scottish and UK benchmarks. It is believed that one contributing factor to this effect is the shift from supporting individual projects to one where the emphasis is on improving the entire ecology of interventions available and joining these up. This has included establishing clear leadership responsibility in an area that has traditionally been "everyone's problem but no one's in particular", introducing shared targets for the city, establishing a Youth Gateway model to promote information sharing and joint service commissioning, and embedding schools into the partnership model.
>
> Young unemployed people were commonly in a "revolving door", between publicly funded projects, which rarely led to positive outcomes. Steps taken to address this have included action to promote improved joint working and bringing in a tracking system. A number of changes to promote genuine collaboration have also been introduced, including establishing a Service Level Agreement in 2009 outlining the roles and responsibilities of all key players

> **Box 4.6. Youth unemployment: Tackling fragmentation in Glasgow, United Kingdom** (cont.)
>
> and the introduction of youth employability groups to monitor progress on the ground – each chaired by a head teacher. Addressing structural difficulties at the departmental level is a long-term goal. Under the banner of Glasgow Works, a co-commissioning model was piloted where funders have adopted a more transparent approach to financing interventions.
>
> Source: OECD (2013), *Local Strategies for Youth Unemployment: Learning from Practice*, OECD Publishing, Paris, www.oecd.org/employment/leed/Local%20Strategies%20for%20Youth%20Employment%20FINAL%20FINAL.pdf.

Recommendation: Urgently focus labour market integration efforts to build inclusive growth and target place-based initiatives to migrants.

Going forward, there are a number of groups in Turkey that face significant labour market challenges which prevent them from finding and sustaining employment. In particular, Turkey is at the forefront of the migration crisis with a significant number of Syrians in the country. There is an opportunity for Turkey play a leadership role in managing the migration crisis through place-based programmes for migrants. However, this requires more effective and comprehensive actions to ensure that migrants receive adequate counselling and support to integrate them in the labour market. Currently, a comprehensive strategy has not been introduced within the employment services. During the OECD study visit, it was noted that the government is developing plans to support migrants in Turkey. However, no specific actions or programmes were observed in either Kocaeli or Trabzon. This process should be urgently expedited and İŞKUR should be at the forefront of delivering employment programmes and social services to these individuals.

Local governments have a critical role to play in working with migrants to develop concrete and innovative programme responses. In Turkey, the national government can play a facilitation role by working with the provinces to identify "what works" and share information among provinces in assisting and helping these groups find sustainable employment. There is no "one-size-fits-all" strategy, which will effectively solve this situation. In this policy area, partnerships are a critical tool to leverage the knowledge, expertise and programme tools of each local player to ensure that they are working towards a common vision for the community. OECD work in this policy area demonstrates that activation and integration services should be provided as soon as possible, and that the integration of poorly educated migrants requires long-term training and support (OECD, 2016a).

While the situation in Turkey is unique in terms of the mass numbers of migrants as well as their demographic and skills profile, Turkey can look at other OECD countries, where local governments have been developing a number of activities to support migrants to achieve labour market success. Box 4.7 provides an example from Italy, which has a national System of Protection for Asylum Seekers and Refugees (SPRAR).

> **Box 4.7. OECD example: Integrating vulnerable migrants**
>
> The national System of Protection for Asylum Seekers and Refugees (SPRAR) established by the Italian Ministry of Interior is managed by the National Association of Italian Municipalities (ANCI) and implemented by municipalities. Third sector organisations also play a prominent role in project delivery.
>
> The municipalities volunteer to participate in SPRAR projects through an annual call. The municipalities can apply to the National Fund for asylum policies and services to develop and implement projects for "integrated reception". Activities associated with "integrated reception" include the initial provision of accommodation and meals, information provision, language courses, access to local services (e.g. social and health assistance), adult education, access to schools for minors, further legal guidance, customised support into employment, self-employment and business creation. The essential features of SPRAR approach are as follows:
>
> - A multi-level governance perspective with strong co-ordination between the Ministry of Interior and the National Association of Italian Municipalities;
> - The decentralisation of "integrated reception" activities;
> - Nationally funded reception projects, which include volunteer service delivery organisations;
> - The prominent role played by the third sector in project implementation;
> - The promotion and development of local networks involving a wide array of actors and stakeholders to ensure the success of reception, protection and inclusion measures.
>
> Source: OECD (2017b, forthcoming), *The integration of vulnerable migrants in small town villages: The case of Italy*, OECD Publishing, Paris.

References

OECD (2017a, forthcoming), *Engaging employers in apprenticeship opportunities at the local level*, OECD Publishing, Paris.

OECD (2017b, forthcoming), *The integration of vulnerable migrants in small town villages: The case of Italy*, OECD Publishing, Paris.

OECD (2016a), *Making Integration Work: Refugees and others in need of protection*, OECD Publishing, Paris, http://dx.doi.org/10.1787/9789264251236-en.

OECD (2016b), "Montréal : Métropole de talent – Pistes d'action pour améliorer l'emploi, l'innovation et les compétences", *OECD LEED Working Paper*, available at www.oecd.org/fr/emploi/leed/montreal-metropole-talent-2016.htm.

OECD (2014a), *Employment and Skills Strategies in the United States*, OECD Reviews on Local Job Creation, OECD Publishing, Paris, http://dx.doi.org/10.1787/9789264209398-en.

OECD (2014b), *Employment and Skills Strategies in Canada*, OECD Reviews on Local Job Creation, OECD Publishing, Paris, http://dx.doi.org/10.1787/9789264209374-en.

OECD (2014c), *Employment and Skills Strategies in Korea*, OECD Publishing, Paris, http://dx.doi.org/10.1787/9789264216563-en.

OECD (2014d), *Job Creation and Local Economic Development*, OECD Publishing, Paris, http://dx.doi.org/10.1787/9789264215009-en.

OECD (2013), *Local Strategies for Youth Unemployment: Learning from Practice*, OECD Publishing, Paris, www.oecd.org/employment/leed/Local%20Strategies%20for%20Youth%20Employment%20FINAL%20FINAL.pdf.

ORGANISATION FOR ECONOMIC CO-OPERATION AND DEVELOPMENT

The OECD is a unique forum where governments work together to address the economic, social and environmental challenges of globalisation. The OECD is also at the forefront of efforts to understand and to help governments respond to new developments and concerns, such as corporate governance, the information economy and the challenges of an ageing population. The Organisation provides a setting where governments can compare policy experiences, seek answers to common problems, identify good practice and work to co-ordinate domestic and international policies.

The OECD member countries are: Australia, Austria, Belgium, Canada, Chile, the Czech Republic, Denmark, Estonia, Finland, France, Germany, Greece, Hungary, Iceland, Ireland, Israel, Italy, Japan, Korea, Latvia, Luxembourg, Mexico, the Netherlands, New Zealand, Norway, Poland, Portugal, the Slovak Republic, Slovenia, Spain, Sweden, Switzerland, Turkey, the United Kingdom and the United States. The European Union takes part in the work of the OECD.

OECD Publishing disseminates widely the results of the Organisation's statistics gathering and research on economic, social and environmental issues, as well as the conventions, guidelines and standards agreed by its members.

www.ingramcontent.com/pod-product-compliance
Lightning Source LLC
Chambersburg PA
CBHW082353220526
45470CB00008B/2728